Lovely Knitted Lace

Lovely Knitted Lace

A Geometric Approach to Gorgeous Wearables

Brooke Nico

LARK

An Imprint of Sterling Publishing
387 Park Avenue South
New York, NY 10016

ISBN 978-1-4547-0781-3

Library of Congress Cataloging-in-Publication Data

Nico, Brooke.
Lovely knitted lace : a geometric approach to gorgeous wearables / Brooke Nico. -- First edition.
p. cm.
Includes index.
ISBN 978-1-4547-0781-3
1. Knitting--Patterns. 2. Knitwear. 3. Shapes. I. Title.
TT825.N487 2014
746.43'2--dc23
2013021581

Distributed in Canada by Sterling Publishing
c/o Canadian Manda Group, 165 Dufferin Street
Toronto, Ontario, Canada M6K 3H6
Distributed in the United Kingdom by GMC Distribution Services
Castle Place, 166 High Street, Lewes, East Sussex, England BN7 1XU
Distributed in Australia by Capricorn Link (Australia) Pty. Ltd.
P.O. Box 704, Windsor, NSW 2756, Australia

For information about custom editions, special sales, and premium and corporate purchases, please contact Sterling Special Sales at 800-805-5489 or specialsales@sterlingpublishing.com.

Email academic@larkbooks.com for information about desk and examination copies. The complete policy can be found at larkcrafts.com.

Manufactured in China

2 4 6 8 10 9 7 5 3 1

larkcrafts.com

contents

Introduction 6
Getting Started 8

triangles 22
Triangle Tulip Shawl 24
Flutter Shawl 30
Poppy Shawl 36
Floral Tunic 40

rectangles 44
Japanese Leaf Scarf/Cables and Lace Stole 46
Butterfly Stole 52
Posies Wrap 56
Starry Nights Bolero 60

circles 64
Angel Shawl/Poinsettia Jacket 66
Traveling Vines Cape/Skirt 76
Orange Crush Beret 82
Camellia Dolman 86

squares 96
Dahlia Shawl 98
Aster Shirt 104
Birch Jacket 108
Moondance Shrug 114

Motifs for Exploration 118

Knitting Abbreviations 126
Knitting Needle Size Chart 127
Yarn Weights 127
About the Author 127
Acknowledgments 128
Index 128

introduction

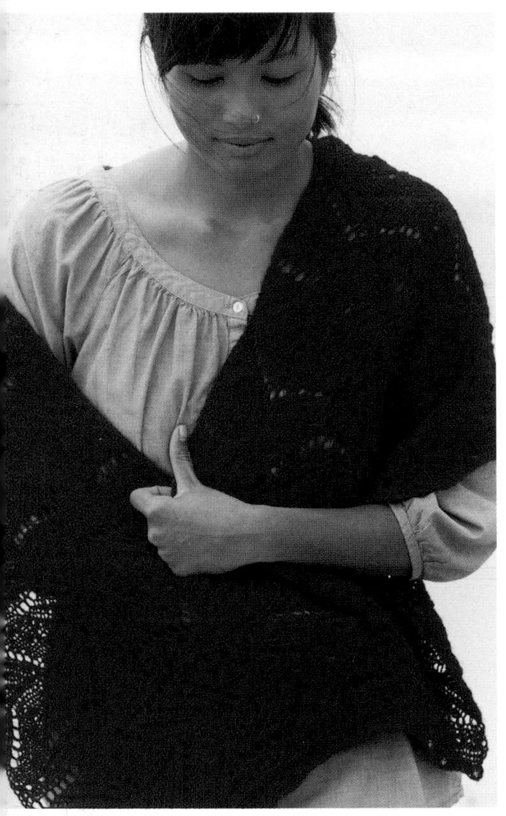

I love knitting lace! It appeals to both sides of the brain. Its logical, mathematical aspect makes the left side of the brain quite happy, while its creative flow sets the right brain on fire. You can find a simple, intuitive lace motif (such as the basic fagoting pattern in the Birch Jacket on page 108) that is easily memorized and quite suitable for knit night or TV knitting, but will still yield beautiful results. Or you can try more challenging motifs, such as the Mock Cable and Japanese Leaf motifs used in the Japanese Leaf Scarf and its Stole variant on page 46. These patterns demand more concentration due to their changing stitch counts and combinations of knits and purls across a row. Regardless of your skill level or challenge preference, lace knitting offers something for everyone—and you'll find projects that suit a variety of needs throughout this book.

The best thing about lace knitting, however, is its economy! Dollars for yardage, lace weight yarns are often the least expensive available. Great lace yarns are relatively inexpensive per 1400yds (128m), and that's plenty of yarn to make a beautiful shawl (which will also yield months of entertaining knitting). In addition, the nature of the lace fabric—in other words, all the holes—means that you get more yardage of fabric with less yarn. The Floral Tunic on page 40 is knit using Scrumptious 4-ply, a yarn that recommends a stockinette stitch gauge of 6 sts per inch (2.5cm). To knit the tunic in stockinette stitch, using the same yarn, would require approximately 2300yds (2102m) for the smallest size. In a lace motif, the pattern requires less than 1200 yds (1097m) for the smallest size!

When I first started knitting lace, I made shawl after shawl. There is, however, a limit to how many shawls one person can own. I quickly decided that I needed to expand my repertoire to garments and other accessories. Knitted lace fabric is richly textured by details; garments with basic shapes and simple construction lines allow those details to shine. This book is the result of my experimentation of turning basic shapes into lovely, wearable garments. Each chapter will take you through a variety of pieces, each made from a defining shape. I've attempted to offer a variety of pieces, with accessories and garments included in each chapter. Lace knitting does not have to be limited to shawls. You'll find several jackets and sweaters, as well as scarves, stoles, and yes, even shawls! In addition, there is a range of skill levels in each chapter. And on page 118, you'll find charts for additional lace motifs. I hope you'll enjoy experimenting with these and perhaps create your own variations of the designs!

getting started

Lace knitting does not require teeny-tiny needles and thread-like yarn!

Yarn

You can knit lace in any size yarn, using any size needles. For example, the Triangle Tulip Shawl pattern (page 24) is written for a worsted weight wool, using a 5.0mm (size 8 U.S.) needle. This yields a cozy shawl, perfect to wear instead of a coat on a brisk fall day. Knitting the same pattern with a lace weight yarn, such as Rowan Fine Lace, on a 3.25mm (size 3 U.S.) needle gives us a very different, but equally lovely, shawl—the perfect addition to a flowing dress. Because this shawl is knit from the top down with triangular shaping, you can work the pattern at any gauge and with any yarn you desire. (Just keep repeating chart 2 on page 29 until it reaches the depth you want, then transition to chart 3.)

Throughout this book, you will see a variety of weights of yarn used, from the worsted weight yarn mentioned above to the fine lace weights in the Flutter Shawl on page 30. For beginning lace knitters, I recommend starting with some of the patterns written for heavier yarns, such as the Triangle Tulip Shawl (page 24), the Posies Wrap (page 56), or the Moondance Shrug (page 114).

When we talk about lace knitting, we're talking about using yarns that will "hold a block." By that, we mean a yarn that has some inherent elasticity and memory. This will open up the holes created by all the yarn overs and allow it to stay stretched after blocking. In other words, some form of animal fiber, wool preferably, is often the best choice for lace knitting. Sometimes, however, the excellent drape of silk or linen is needed to achieve the garment's desired movement or flow. In the case of the Aster Shirt in the Squares chapter (page 104), I chose to use Fiesta Yarns

Linnette for several reasons. I wanted a lightweight garment, suitable for warm-weather wear. In addition, the garment requires drape in order to allow the side panels to move and flow. The stitch pattern in the design is extremely structural, and the addition of the twisted stitches and mock cables lends stability to the resulting fabric. This will counteract the tendency of linen and cotton to stretch, yet still allow for the desired drape. Likewise, the Floral Tunic in the Triangles chapter (page 40) is made with a silk/wool blend. In the past several years, we have seen a huge increase in the amount of blended yarns such as this. Blending fibers in a yarn allows us to gain the advantage of each fiber, while counteracting the negatives. Silk is a wonderfully flowing fiber with great drape. It also has little memory and stretches exponentially! Wool, on the other hand, has little drape, but is extremely elastic. When we combine the two, we get a fabric with drape and movement, but also elasticity and memory—the perfect fabric for this garment!

Gauge

One of the most hated words in knitting…gauge. Unfortunately, a gauge swatch is absolutely essential in all knitting, including lace knitting. But switching your approach to doing the swatch may make it more enjoyable! The gauge swatch offers your first opportunity to play with your yarn and stitch pattern. Working the gauge swatch is a chance to try out the stitches in a relaxed manner, figuring out how all those yarn overs and decreases line up, which will make the pattern much easier. Don't think of the swatch as a chore, but as an opportunity for play!

Gauge, simply put, is the mathematical relationship of stitches and rows to a specific number of inches. Throughout this book, you will see gauge listed in one of two methods. If the pattern has several lace motifs, I have measured the gauge over stockinette or garter stitch over 4 inches (10cm) square. If the pattern has one predominate lace motif, I have measured the gauge over one or several repeats of that motif, which will give you a measurement not necessarily 4 inches (10cm) square. In either case, the gauge swatch is measured over a swatch after blocking. Wash your swatch and pin it out to block as you would the finished garment. Let the swatch dry completely, and then unpin it. After unpinning the swatch, I like to let it rest for several hours, allowing the swatch to relax to a more natural gauge.

There are two categories of gauge. One is the pattern gauge, or the gauge stated in the introduction of a pattern. The pattern will state, for example, 18 sts/22 rows = 4"/10cm over stitch pattern using 4.5mm (size 7 U.S.) needles. What this means is that the designer used size 7 needles to get that particular gauge. That does not mean that you will necessarily use size 7 needles! This brings us to the second category of gauge, which is the knitter's gauge, or the gauge that you get when knitting your yarn with your selected needles. You may find that a 4.5mm (size 7 U.S.) needle gives you a gauge of 20 sts = 4"/10cm. What that means is that your individual stitches are smaller, giving you more stitches in each inch (2.5cm). You need to make each stitch a little bit bigger; therefore, you need to use a bigger needle in order to reach the specified pattern gauge.

The pattern gauge means that all of the math in that pattern is based on that specific relationship of stitches per inch (2.5cm). For example, the Floral Tunic in the Triangles chapter (page 40) has a pattern gauge of 18 sts/22 rows = 4"/10cm, or 4.5 sts = 1"/2.5cm. The size Small has a chest measurement of 44 inches (112cm). Multiply 44 by 4.5 stitches per inch (2.5cm) and we get 198 stitches. With this particular lace motif, we need a stitch repeat of 8 stitches, which gives us a total of 200 stitches at the chest. If you want to have a finished garment with a chest of 44 inches (112cm), your knitter's gauge must be the same as the pattern gauge of 18 sts = 4"/10cm. If your gauge is a little smaller, say, 20 sts = 4"/10cm, or 5 sts per 1"/2.5cm, then your finished garment will have a chest measurement of 200 (stitches at chest) divided by 5 (stitches per inch [2.5cm]) or 40 inches (102cm), and consequently will probably be too small.

Lace knitting is extremely flexible and stretchy. Quite often, you can block it to almost any gauge you desire. The question when evaluating your gauge swatch is, do you like the resulting fabric at that gauge? If you

are knitting a shawl or other accessory, and the exact finished measurement is not essential to the fit, then you can swatch to find a fabric that you like, rather than to a specific measurement.

The Butterfly Stole, in the Rectangles chapter (page 52), has a pattern gauge of 32 sts/34 rows = 4"/10cm, which breaks down to 8 sts = 1"/2.5cm. I used a 3.75mm (size 5 U.S.) needle to achieve that pattern gauge. In order to get a finished stole 13 inches (33cm) wide, we need to cast on 104 stitches. But say you have a cobweb weight yarn in your stash and want to work the stole in it. After working a gauge swatch, you discover that this yarn worked at the pattern gauge looks too loose and sloppy. However, worked at a tighter gauge of 36 sts = 4"/10cm, or 9 sts = 1"/2.5cm, it looks quite lovely!

At this point you have several options: 1) find a different yarn that works at the pattern gauge, 2) work the pattern as written, or 3) adjust the pattern. If you choose option 2, just be aware that your finished measurements will be a function of your gauge. The finished width of your stole will be 104 stitches divided by 9 sts = 1"/2.5cm, or 11.5 inches (29cm) wide. You will also need to work more rows to achieve the target length, which means that you will need more yarn than the pattern requirements.

If, however, you want the finished stole to be closer to the 13 inches (33cm) width, then you will need to choose option 3, and adjust the pattern. This is going to require some math, but rest assured—it's all third-grade math! In order to get a 13-inch (33cm) width, you multiply 13 by 9 (stitches per inch [2.5cm]), which is 117 stitches. The stitch pattern is a multiple of 14 stitches (the highlighted stitches on the chart, page 000), with a total of 6 stitches at the edges (the stitches outside the highlight). In knitting terms, this is stated as a multiple of 14 stitches + 6. The easiest way to figure out the number of stitches to cast on for your gauge is to try adding just one repeat of the stitch pattern to the pattern. So, 104 (the pattern recommended cast on) + 14 (one repeat of the motif) = 118 stitches, which is nice and close to the target stitch count of 117 stitches! If you cast on 118 stitches, and work the pattern as written, working 8 repeats of the pattern motif across, you will have a finished stole about 13 inches (33cm) wide. Again, remember that you are now working more stitches in each row, and will need to work more rows to achieve length—and will therefore need more yarn!

charts

Several of the patterns in this book include written line-by-line instructions. However, almost all of the patterns have charts, so you can work the projects either way you'd like. If you're a beginner, I'd encourage you to start with projects such as the Triangle Tulip Shawl, the Posies Wrap, and the Moondance Shrug. But whatever your skill level, I encourage you to try working the charts. Charts give the knitter a huge advantage in lace knitting. In written words, you get a string of letters, with lots of k's, which are often difficult to interpret. The eye may jump over and skip an important piece of information, which will then lead to adult words and ripping! Charts, however, give you a clear picture of your knitting.

Take, for example, the following stitch pattern:

Row 1: K2tog, k4, yo, k1, yo, k4, ssk.
Row 2 and all WS rows: Purl.
Row 3: K2tog, (k3, yo) 2 times, k3, ssk.
Row 5: K2tog, k2, yo, k5, yo, k2, ssk.
Row 7: K2tog, k1, yo, k7, yo, k1, ssk.
Row 9: K2tog, yo, k9, yo, k2tog.
Row 11: K1, yo, k4, sk2p, k4, yo, k1.
Row 13: K2, yo, k3, sk2p, k3, yo, k2.
Row 15: K3, yo, k2, sk2p, k2, yo, k3.
Row 17: K4, yo, k1, sk2p, k1, yo, k4.
Row 19: K5, yo, sk2p, yo, k5.

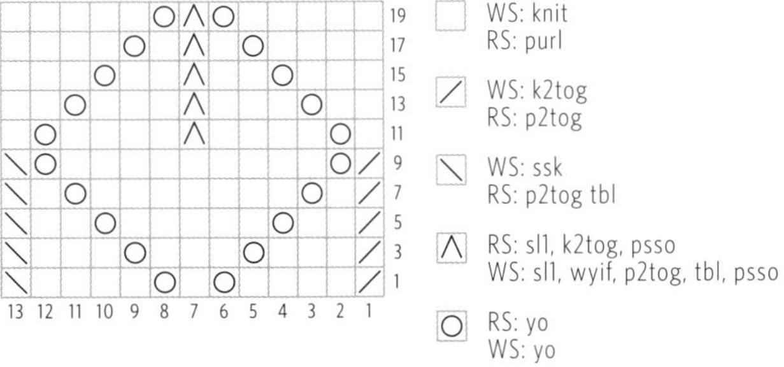

The words alone give you no picture of what you are knitting! Compare that to the chart above for the same stitch pattern, and you know right away that you are creating a diamond outlined by yarn overs.

The other advantage of charts is that they tell you not only which stitches you are knitting but also where those stitches lie in relationship to the rows below. Row 3, for example, tells you that stitches 6, 7, and 8 are all knits. But you also know that stitches 6 and 8 should be on top of the yarn overs from row 1. This will help you identify and correct mistakes quickly and easily. If you are knitting row 3 and find that stitch 6 is not sitting on top of the yarn over from row 1, then you know right away that you have made an error and need to find it before you go any further.

Working a lace chart is easy—you just need to know the code!

1. Charts are read from right to left on right-side rows, from left to right on wrong-side rows.

2. The row numbers are placed on the side of the chart where you will begin the row. In other words, right-side rows are numbered on the right edge, wrong-side rows are numbered on the left edge. If numbers are only given along the right side and they are all odd numbers, then only right-side rows are charted; all wrong-side rows are knit (or purl) across. In the chart at left, therefore, only right-side rows are charted, and are numbered 1, 3, 5, and so on, up the right edge of the chart.

3. Charts are always written from the perspective of the public (right) side of the knitting.

4. Charts will be accompanied by a legend, which will tell you what each symbol means. Be sure to take note of what each symbol means on the right-side and the wrong-side rows.

5. Charts are a picture. When you read a row of written instructions, you are translating the words into a picture, then the picture into an action. When you read a chart, you need only translate the picture into an action. Also, quite often that picture clearly represents the action, as in the symbols for k2tog (/) and ssk (\). When you do a k2tog, note that you insert your right needle into the two stitches from left to right, just as the symbol is a slash moving from left to right.

6. Charts clearly tell you where each stitch lies in relation to the row below.

7. Charts help you see the patterns, see where the stitches are going to line up, and predict what comes next.

When a stitch pattern has a changing stitch count, you may come across a "no stitch" square, which is signified with a gray square. This means exactly what it says—there is no stitch in that space, and there is no stitch on your needle. Just skip over that space, and move on to the next square in the chart. For example, in the Water Lilies chart on page 123, row 5 includes a 7 out of 3 increase. In this stitch, you work (k3tog tbl, yo) three times, k3tog tbl, all into the same three stitches. This gives you four new stitches. We need spaces for those four stitches on subsequent rows, and in order to keep the picture of the motif intact, those spaces need to be in the middle of the chart. So, I have placed "no stitch" squares in row 1 as placeholders for those stitches until they appear on row 7. Row 1 is worked as follows: Yo, k1, yo, ssk, k11, k2tog, yo, k1, yo, ignoring the "no stitch" squares.

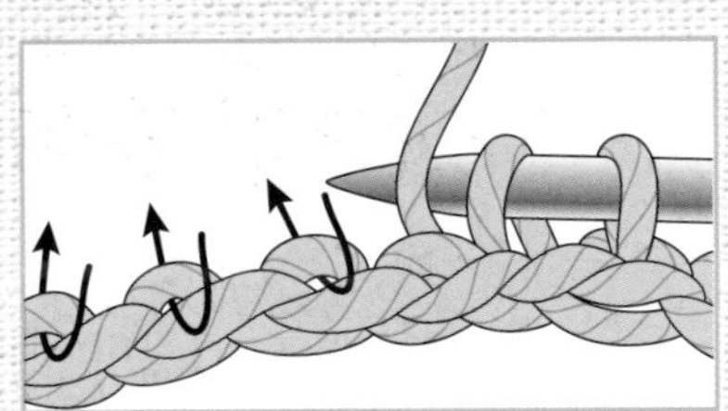

Techniques

Provisional Cast On

Several of the patterns in this book, including the Orange Crush Beret on page 82, call for a provisional cast on. The provisional cast on allows the knitter to at some point remove the cast on and have live stitches, rather than picking up and knitting into the cast on edge, which will give you a bulky seam. To work a provisional cast on, you will need a crochet hook, smooth waste yarn (preferably cotton), and your knitting needle and working yarn. Start by crocheting a chain with the waste yarn. Chain five to seven more stitches than the cast on calls for. Fasten off and cut the waste yarn. If you look closely at your crochet chain, you will see that from the front, each chain looks like a knit stitch. Turn it to the back and you will see what looks like a purl bump on the back of each chain. With your working needle and yarn, pick up and knit one stitch in the bump of each crochet chain, until you have picked up the correct number of stitches called for in the pattern. The five to seven extra chains are there just in case you counted wrong initially and will just hang down. When you are ready to use those stitches, you can simply unzip that crochet chain and live stitches will appear, ready to be knit!

Belly Button Cast On

The Angel Shawl (page 66) and Dahlia Shawl (page 98)are two patterns in this book that are worked from the center out. These will require you to cast on four to eight stitches, usually on double-pointed needles (DPNs), then join to work in the round. This can be incredibly fiddly. With only a few stitches on each needle, the double points want to flip around, which makes joining without twisting an added challenge. The belly button cast on is a great trick to alleviate these problems. You will need smooth waste yarn (preferably cotton) in a gauge similar to your working yarn. With the waste yarn, cast on the required number of stitches to one double-pointed needle. Work 2 to 4 inches (5.1 to 10.2cm) of I-cord as follows:

Knit across all stitches. *Do not turn work. Slide the stitches to the other end of the needle, and knit across all stitches. Repeat from *. You will always have the knit side of the fabric facing you; the working yarn will stretch across the back of the knitting and will eventually cause the knitting to roll into a tube.

After you have worked at least 2 inches (5.1cm) of I-cord, divide the stitches evenly onto two needles. We'll pretend we cast on eight stitches, so you will have four stitches on each needle. Fold the tube flat, so the needles are sitting parallel to each other, with the right side out. Join your working yarn and knit across the four stitches on one needle, flip the work around, and, with a new DPN, knit across the stitches on the second needle. You will still have the stitches divided on two needles. You have now worked round 1 of the pattern. You can continue in this way, working the pattern on only two DPNs, for a few rounds, until you have worked one or two increase rounds. Now you will need to divide the stitches onto more double-pointed needles or onto a circular needle as the pattern calls for, but you will have enough fabric to feel confident doing so. At some point, you will cut out the waste yarn, thread the live stitches with the tail of the working yarn, and pull the hole closed. You can wait until you are ready to block your garment, or you can do it after working a few inches. I prefer to do it sooner rather than later, so I can pat myself on the back and admire my beautiful cast on!

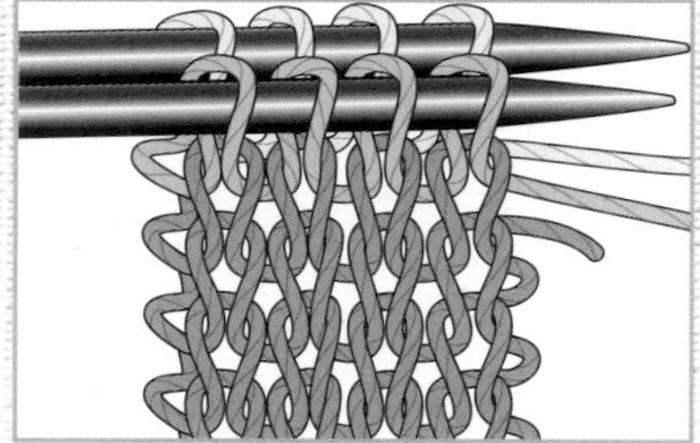

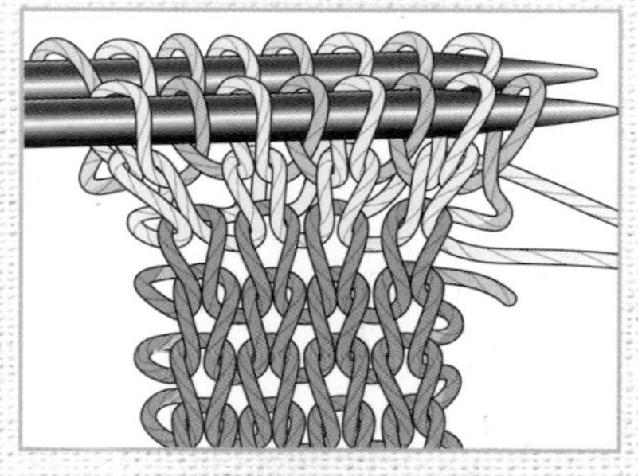

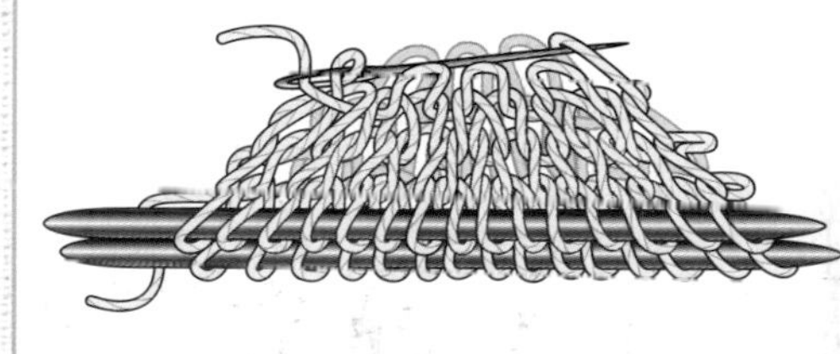

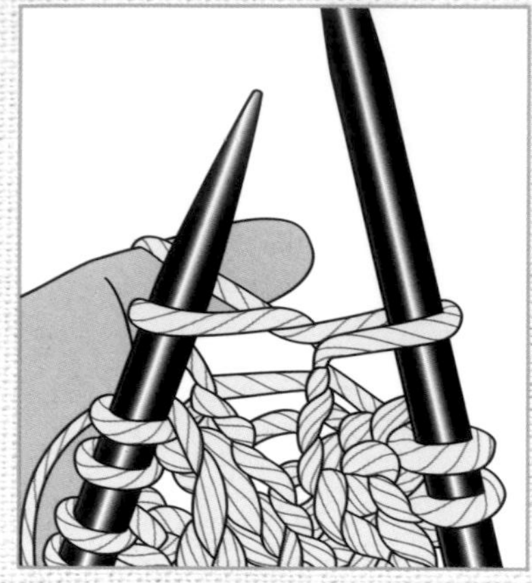

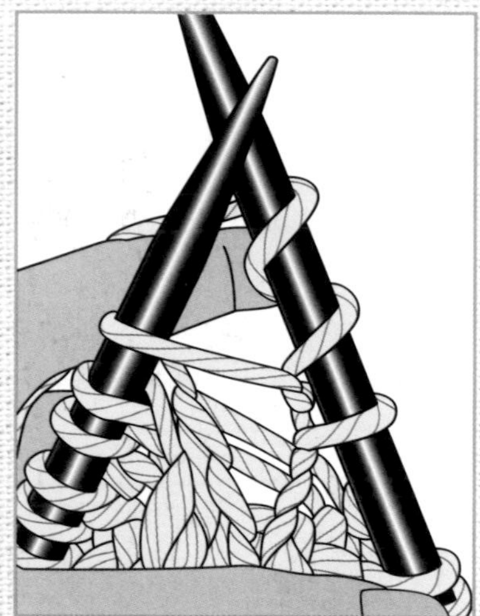

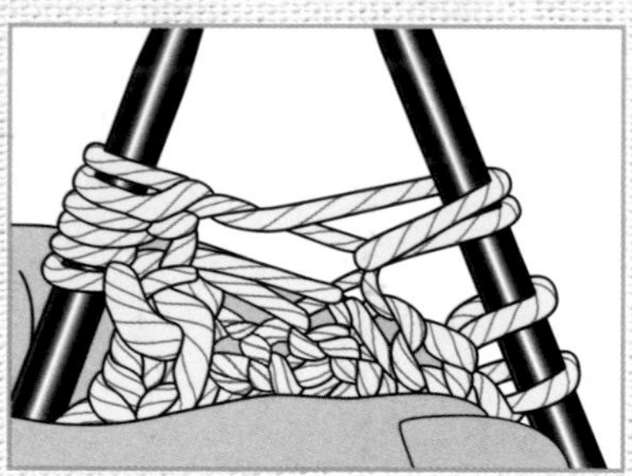

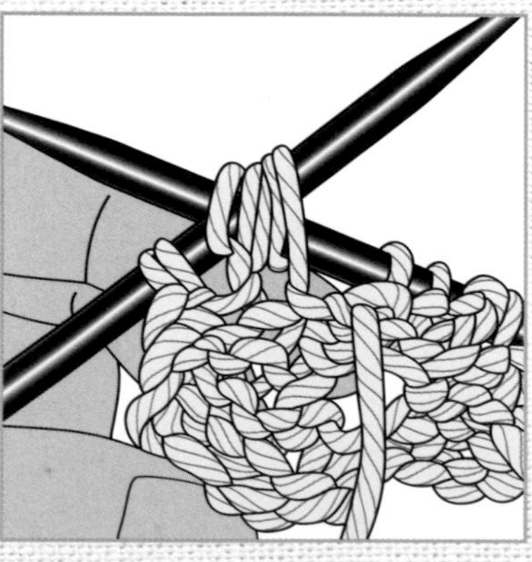

Nupps

Nupps are a textural embellishment found frequently in Estonian lace work. You can find nupps in designs such as the Flutter Shawl (page 30) and Floral Tunic (page 40). A nupp is similar to a bobble, but tends to sit within the knitted fabric and looks more like a flower bud. To make a nupp, you will work five, seven, or nine stitches out of one stitch. On the following row, these five, seven, or nine stitches are worked together, thus taking you back to the original count of one stitch.

For a seven-stitch nupp, for example, you will work up to the nupp placement:

* Insert your needle into the next stitch and knit it, *do not drop the stitch off the left-hand needle*, yo, and repeat from * two times more. Insert your needle into the stitch and knit it once more; now drop the stitch off the left-hand needle. You have worked (k1, yo) three times, k1 into the same stitch, thus making seven stitches out of one. Continue across the row as charted. On the next row, when you come to these seven stitches, p7tog if working flat, or k7tog through the back loop if working in the round, which will create the nupp.

There are a few simple tricks to make your nupps easier to work. The looser you can work the initial seven stitches, the easier it will be to work them together on the return row. To that end, I like to elongate those seven stitches a little, as follows:

* Insert your needle into the next stitch and knit it, *do not drop the stitch off the left-hand needle*, yo 2x, and repeat from * two times more. Insert your needle into the stitch and knit it once more; now drop the stitch off the left-hand needle. You have made 10 stitches out of one. On the return row, when you get to these 10 stitches, you will slip them purlwise, one at a time, to the right-hand needle, dropping the extra wraps of each yarn over when you come to them. In other words, you will *slip 1 knit stitch, slip 1 yo, drop 1 yo * three times, slip last knit stitch.

Now you have seven nupp stitches that you can slip back to the left-hand needle and purl or knit together. The dropped yarn overs will elongate each of the seven stitches a little bit, and will make it much easier to work them together!

If you find you really just hate doing the nupps, then don't do them! Knitting is supposed to be fun, remember? You can replace the nupp with a bead if you wish, or just leave it out altogether. Both options will give you a different look, and you can decide whether you like it during the swatching process.

Short Rows

The Traveling Vines Cape/Skirt (page 76) in the Circles chapter is shaped using short rows. Short rows is a technique that is used to create wedges in a knitted fabric. In essence, you are doing exactly what the name suggests—knitting a "short row." Take, for example, a piece of knitting where you have 20 stitches on your needles. To work a short row, you would work a designated number of stitches as outlined in the pattern. In this example, we'll say knit 15. This will leave five stitches remaining on your left needle, which you will not work. If, however, you simply turn your work, leaving the five stitches unworked, and begin working the next row back, you will leave a big hole at the point of the turn. In any row of knitting, each stitch should be connected to the stitches on either side of it. So, before turning your work and starting the next row, you need to connect the 15th stitch knitted with the 16th stitch, which will be left unworked. This is called a *wrap and turn*, or w&t.

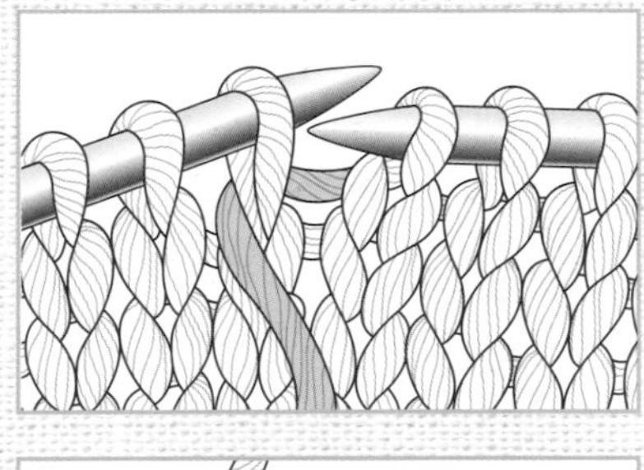

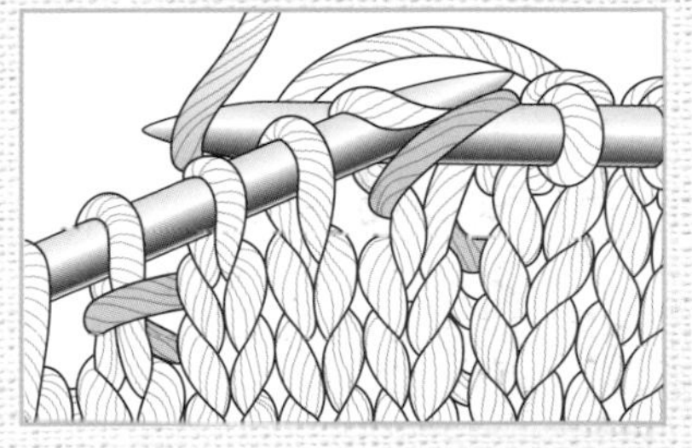

Here's how to work a w&t:

- **w&t after a knit stitch:** Knit the required stitches, then slip the next stitch purlwise to the right-hand needle. Bring the yarn to the front between the needles (wrapping the slipped stitch), slip the stitch back to the left-hand needle, and bring the yarn to the back. Turn work.
- **w&t after a purl stitch:** Purl the required stitches, then slip the next stitch purlwise to the right-hand needle. Bring the yarn to the back between the needles (wrapping the slipped stitch), slip the stitch back to the left-hand needle, and bring the yarn to the front. Turn work.

You will notice that the wrap will appear to be a purl bump on the right side of the fabric. Because the stitch pattern in the cape pattern is a combination of stockinette stitch and reverse stockinette stitch, those wraps will blend in with the purl bumps.

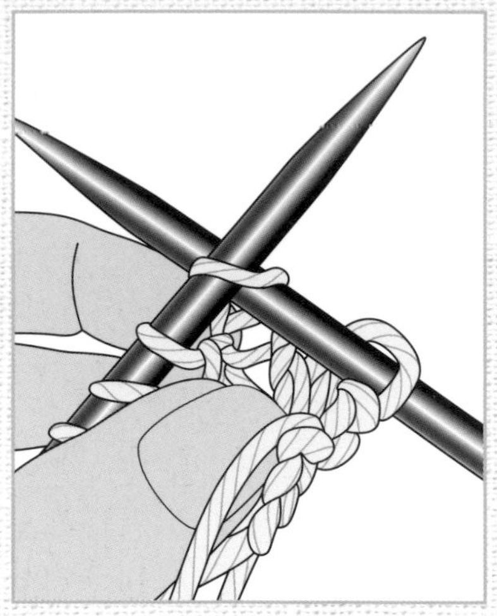

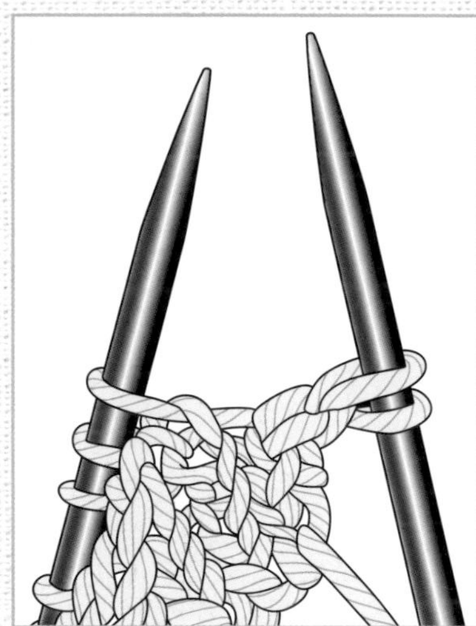

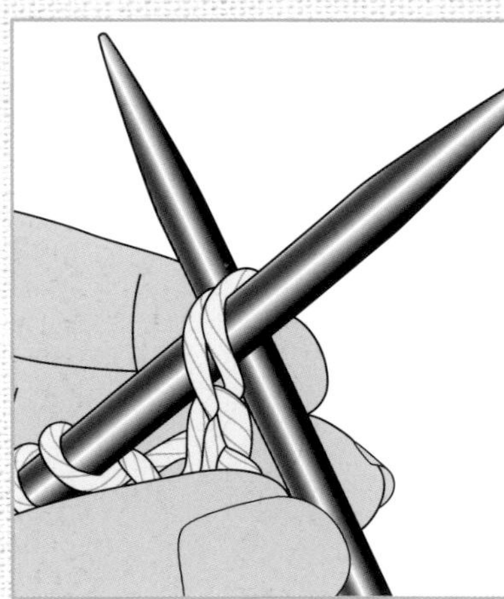

Lace Bind Off

Lace knitting is extremely flexible, and therefore sometimes requires a stretchier than normal bind off. I like to use the lace bind off, otherwise known as a decrease bind off. This bind off essentially will add an extra little chain between the bind-off stitches. This chain can pop up if needed to stretch the fabric, but if it is not needed, it will hide just under the bind off.

To work the lace bind off, knit two stitches. *Slip these two stitches back to the left-hand needle and knit them together through the back loop. You now have one stitch on your right-hand needle. Knit one stitch, which puts you back to two stitches on the right needle. Repeat from * across, until you have worked all stitches off the left-hand needle. Fasten off the last stitch as usual.

Fixing Mistakes in Lace Knitting

It's inevitable: mistakes are going to happen at some point. The goal is to minimize them and to catch them quickly. The first line of defense is to use stitch markers liberally! I place a marker between each repeat of my motif, using different color markers to identify key sections (for example, the center spine stitch of a triangle shawl). If, for example, you are working the Cables and Lace Stole (page 50) in the Rectangles chapter, you will place a marker in between each repeat of the motif across the row. On each return row as you are working back, count the stitches in between each marker to make sure you have the correct number. It is much easier to find the one missing stitch in a group of 18 than it is to locate a missing stitch out of 235 stitches!

Another way to minimize errors is to take the time to actually look at your knitting. Quite often, we get absorbed in the process of making each stitch, getting across each row, and we don't take the time to look at the piece as a whole. Take a break every three or four rows, spread out the piece on the needles, and admire the lovely lace fabric you are creating! At the same time, check to make sure that everything looks as it should.

When you do find a mistake, chances are it is probably a missed yarn over. That's an easy fix, especially if you have caught it right away. Let's say you are purling back a return row and discover that the next stitch you should be working is a yarn over, but it's not there! Spread the two needles apart. See the bar of yarn that is stretched between the needles? That's your missing yarn over. Insert the left needle from front to back under that bar. You have recovered the yarn over and can now purl it as needed.

The second most common mistake is a decrease in the wrong place, or a missed decrease. This is also an easy fix. The first rule is to always fix your stitches from the right side of the work, so you can make sure it looks correct! Drop the two stitches that should have been decreased. Insert your crochet hook into those stitches, for a k2tog from left to right, or for a ssk from right to left. With the hook, grasp the strand of yarn that is running behind the stitches (this is called the ladder), and pull through both stitches. You have now re-created your decrease and can put the resulting stitch back on the needles. One rule is important to remember: you cannot fix a mistake next to a yarn over without first dropping the yarn over. The yarn over causes the ladders to twist around each other, making it difficult to determine which ladder is the correct one to use. So, drop the yarn over, fix the decrease, and then rework the yarn over.

For mistakes involving more than one or two stitches, or errors several rows back, it is usually easier and quicker to just rip back a larger section and re-knit it. That does not mean that you need to rip out several rows of knitting, especially if you have several hundred stitches in a row! Isolate the entire repeat of the lace motif that contains the error. Drop that entire repeat off the needles, and unravel down to one row below the mistake. If, for example, you had 10 stitches in a repeat, you will drop that repeat down, let's say, 12 rows. You will now have 10 stitches and 12 spaghetti-like ladders. Place the 10 stitches on a double-pointed needle, and rework the 12 rows using your double-pointed needles. The ladders will be your working yarn. Take time to make sure that with each row you are knitting with the lowest ladder!

triangles

A TRIANGLE IS DEFINED as a polygon of three sides and three angles. The angles within any triangle will always total 180°. This makes the triangle the strongest of polygons and therefore a building block in architecture and art. In architecture, triangles are used to add strength and stability to structures, as well as for aesthetic value. Think of the Sears Tower in Chicago and of course the great pyramids of Egypt. In art, imaginary triangles are used for composition, to draw the viewer in by placing subjects within its boundaries. In fashion, there are many garments that are based on the humble triangle and its variations.

triangle tulip shawl

This design is knit from the top down and is actually two right triangles. For this shawl, I chose Universal Yarns Deluxe Worsted. This is a 100 percent wool yarn in a worsted weight. It has excellent stitch definition and will show off any textural stitch pattern. As an added benefit, because this is a worsted weight, it is knit at a much larger gauge than typical lace shawls, yielding a wonderfully warm shawl! Because the entire pattern is based on ratios, however, you can knit it in any yarn you choose, and at any gauge you choose. To learn more about knitting right triangles, see page 26.

FINISHED MEASUREMENTS

Wingspan 60"/152.5cm
Depth to point 27"/68.5cm

MATERIALS AND TOOLS

Universal Yarns Deluxe Worsted (100% wool; 3.5oz/100g = 220yds/200m): 2 skeins, color #12236—approx 440yds/402.5m of light worsted weight yarn (3)

Knitting needles: 5mm (size 8 U.S.) 24" and 40" circular needles or size to obtain gauge

Stitch markers

Tapestry needle

GAUGE

1 repeat of highlighted sts in chart 2 (10 sts/20 rows) = 3"/7.5cm wide x 3.5"/9cm tall

Always take time to check your gauge.

Notes

Shawl is knit from the top down. Begin with a stockinette stitch tab, into which you will pick up stitches for a 3-stitch stockinette stitch border and the shawl body. Increases are worked at the beginning and end and on each side of the center spine on each right-side row.

Only odd-numbered rows are charted, all even-numbered rows are purl across.

blocking

I like to soak my shawls in a little conditioner before blocking to soften them. My rule of thumb is, if I'll put it on my hair, I can put it on animal hair. After washing and rinsing my shawl, I soak it in a solution of conditioner (just a dab) and tepid water. Let it soak for 15 to 30 minutes, then rinse lightly. The conditioner softens and adds a little shine to your knitting!

working a right triangle

A right triangle is shaped by increasing at the beginning and end of every right-side row. So, to increase for a triangle shawl composed of two right triangles, you will increase at the beginning and end, as well as on either side of a center stitch (or stitches), of each right-side row.

A top-down triangle shawl starts with a small tab (the pink rectangle in the schematic below) at the top center. Through the magic of knitting, this tab will become the edge stitches for the sides of the shawl (the blue sections in the triangle). The center spine can be one or more stitches, and the white areas are your canvas for a lace pattern.

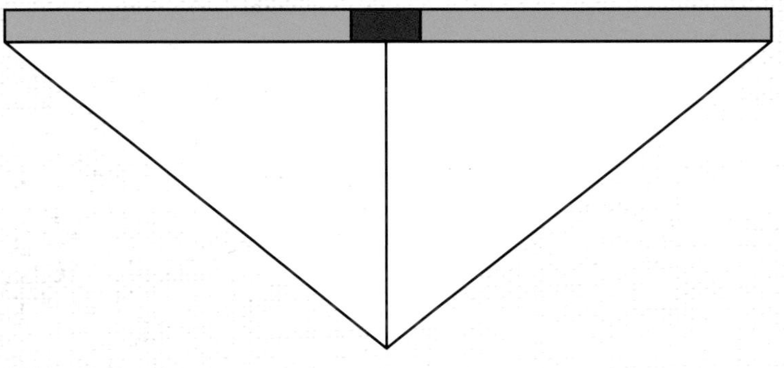

yarn and gauge

The Triangle Tulip Shawl can be knit in any gauge or yarn you choose, depending on the look and feel you want for the project. The sample shown here, for example, is knit in Rowan Fine Lace, an 80% alpaca, 20% merino lace weight yarn. As you can see, you will need to work many more repeats of chart 2 (on page 28) to get a comparably sized shawl, but you can transition to chart 3 (on page 28) after any complete repeat of chart 2, regardless of your gauge.

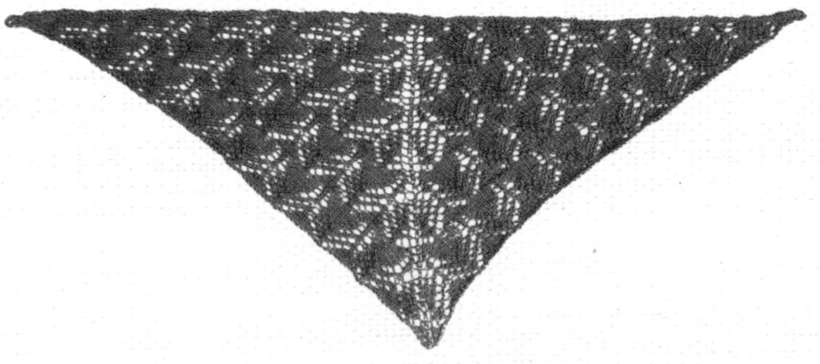

INSTRUCTIONS

tab

Cast on 4 sts. Beginning with WS (purl) row, work 5 rows in St st.

Next row (RS): K4, do not turn, pick up 3 sts in selvedge, pick up 4 sts in cast on edge—11 sts.

Set-up row: P4, PM, (p1, PM) 3 times, p4.

Work chart 1 rows 1–30 once—71 sts.

Work chart 2 rows 1–20 three times, then work chart 2 rows 1–18 once, repeating highlighted sts as needed to markers—227 sts.

Next row (RS): K3, yo, k2tog, yo, k7, (yo, sk2p, yo, k7) repeat to last 5 sts, removing center 2 markers when you come to them, end yo, ssk, yo, k3—229 sts.

Next row: Purl across.

Work chart 3 rows 1–15 over all sts. Repeat highlighted sts 21 times to end of row. Bind off loosely using purl lace bind off on row 16.

FINISHING

Weave in all ends.

Block piece to measurements.

Triangle Tulip Shawl Chart 1

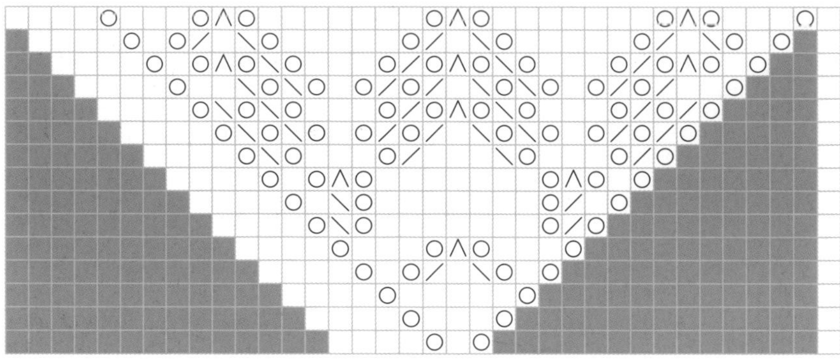

chart continues across page

Triangle Tulip Shawl Chart 2

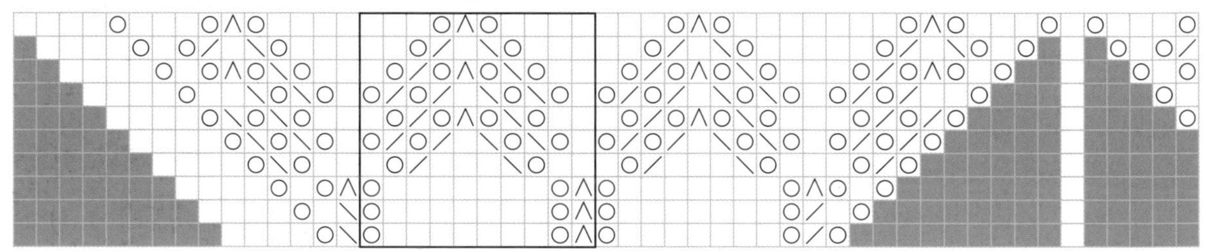

chart continues across page

Triangle Tulip Shawl Chart 3

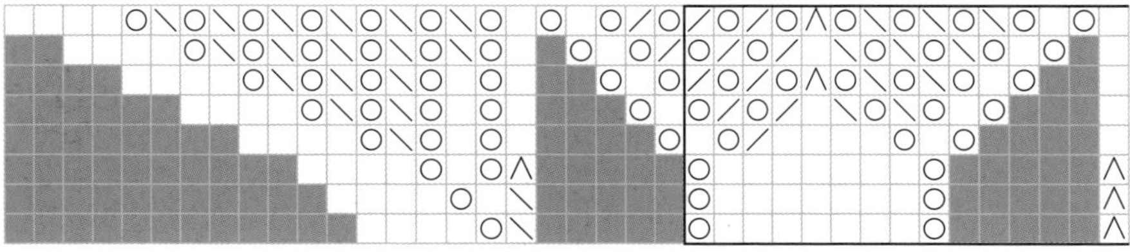

chart continues across page

Only odd-numbered rows are charted; all even-numbered rows are purl across.

Triangle Tulip Shawl Chart 1, continued

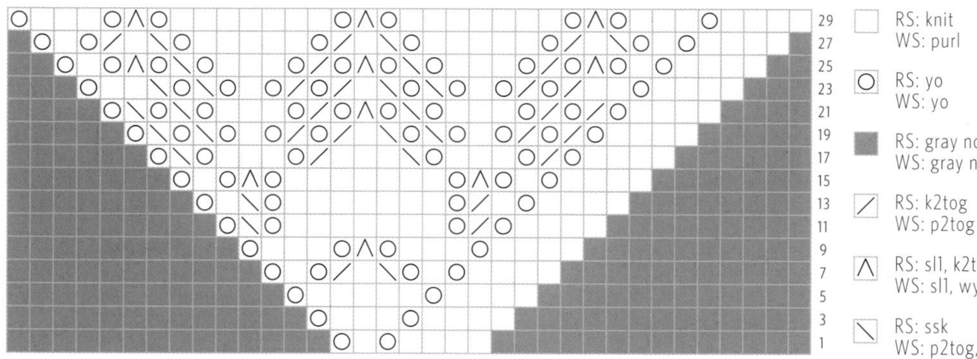

RS: knit
WS: purl

RS: yo
WS: yo

RS: gray no stitch
WS: gray no stitch

RS: k2tog
WS: p2tog

RS: sl1, k2tog, psso
WS: sl1, wyif, p2tog, tbl, psso

RS: ssk
WS: p2tog, tbl

Triangle Tulip Shawl Chart 2, continued

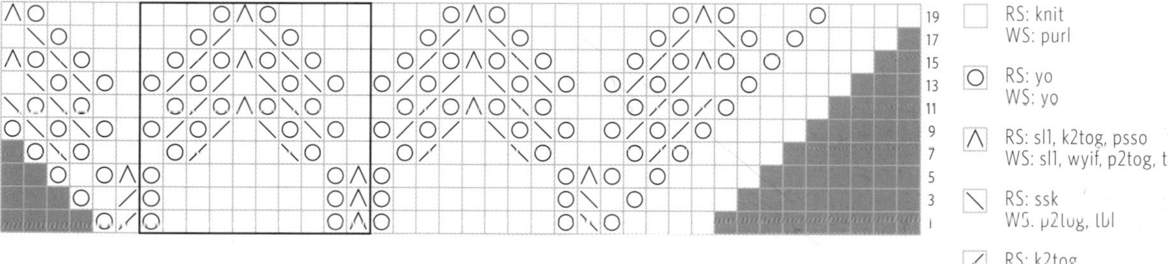

RS: knit
WS: purl

RS: yo
WS: yo

RS: sl1, k2tog, psso
WS: sl1, wyif, p2tog, tbl, psso

RS: ssk
WS: p2tog, tbl

RS: k2tog
WS: p2tog

RS: gray no stitch
WS: gray no stitch

repeat

Triangle Tulip Shawl Chart 3, continued

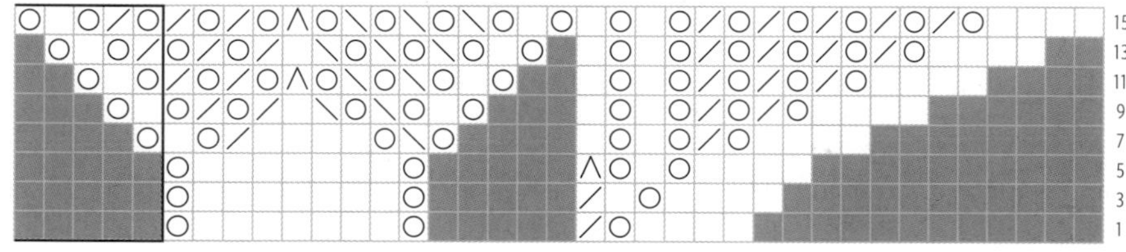

RS: knit
WS: purl

RS: yo
WS: yo

RS: gray no stitch
WS: gray no stitch

RS: ssk
WS: p2tog, tbl

RS: sl1, k2tog, psso
WS: sl1, wyif, p2tog, tbl, psso

RS: k2tog
WS: p2tog

repeat

flutter shawl

A LONGER, NARROWER TRIANGLE HAS BECOME a popular shawl shape lately. It lends itself to a variety of uses. It can be wrapped multiple times around the neck as a scarf, or draped down the front of a jacket as a lapel. Because it is knit side to side, it is a great shawl for those smaller skeins of yarn, or for when you aren't sure how much yarn you have! You will simply increase until you have used up half your yarn, and then begin decreasing for the second half of the shawl.

When I was fortunate enough to find myself with a skein of Flutter, from Black Bunny Fibers, I knew it was the perfect yarn for this shawl. Lightweight, with a bit of shine and drape, it has the ethereal quality I envisioned for this piece. I began swatching, which is my favorite part of the design process. There were several things I wanted to keep in mind as I worked out this design. Because this shawl is knit side to side, I was excited to be able to knit the lower and upper borders along with the body of the shawl. The beautiful color variation of the dye meant that I needed to keep the lace pattern fairly simple and clean (see box, page 32). Because of the silk/merino blend of the yarn, I would have subtle stitch definition, so fagoting would be a beautiful addition to the overall motif of the shawl.

After working several swatches, I hit upon this Estonian variation of a leaf motif. Each leaf is outlined with rows of fagoting but has large sections of stockinette within. The motif for the lower border mirrors this fagoting. I also loved the juxtaposition of the hourglass shape of the leaves with the angular construction of the triangle shawl. In addition, because it is knit side to side, this is a motif that reads well from any direction.

FINISHED MEASUREMENTS

56"/142cm wingspan

MATERIALS AND TOOLS

Black Bunny Fibers Flutter Laceweight (80% superfine merino, 20% silk; 3.5oz/100g = 1300yds/1188.5m): 1 ball, color Red Rain—approx 750yds/686m of fingering weight yarn (0)

Knitting needles: 2.75mm (size 2 U.S.) or size to obtain gauge

Stitch markers

Tapestry needle

GAUGE

1 repeat of highlighted section in chart 2 (22 sts/38 rows) = 3"/7.5cm wide x 4"/10cm tall

Always take time to check your gauge.

Notes

7-stitch nupps are used throughout.

Only odd-numbered rows are charted; all even-numbered rows are purl across.

INSTRUCTIONS

Cast on 17 sts.

SET-UP ROW (WS): p5, PM, p to end.

Work chart 1 rows 1–40 once, working across all sts.

Work chart 2 rows 1–40 six times, repeating highlighted sts as needed as sts increase.

Work chart 3 rows 1–40 six times, repeating highlighted sts as needed as sts decrease.

Work chart 4 rows 1–40 once.

Bind off all sts.

FINISHING

Weave in ends.

Block piece to measurements.

hand-dyed yarns

Hand-dyed yarns can be used for lace; however, you should keep in mind a few tips.

1. Try to stick with dyes that are tonal or have more subtle color changes.

2. Using a lace pattern with more fields of stockinette or garter stitch will minimize visual confusion.

3. Highly textural stitch patterns, such as cables or cross stitches, are not recommended.

Flutter Shawl Chart 1

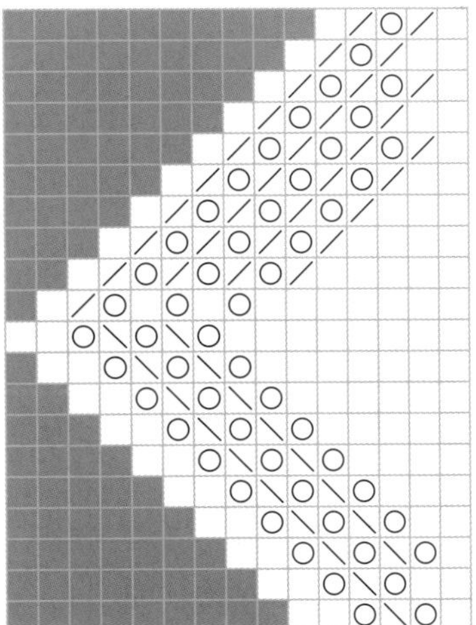

chart continues across page

Flutter Shawl Chart 2

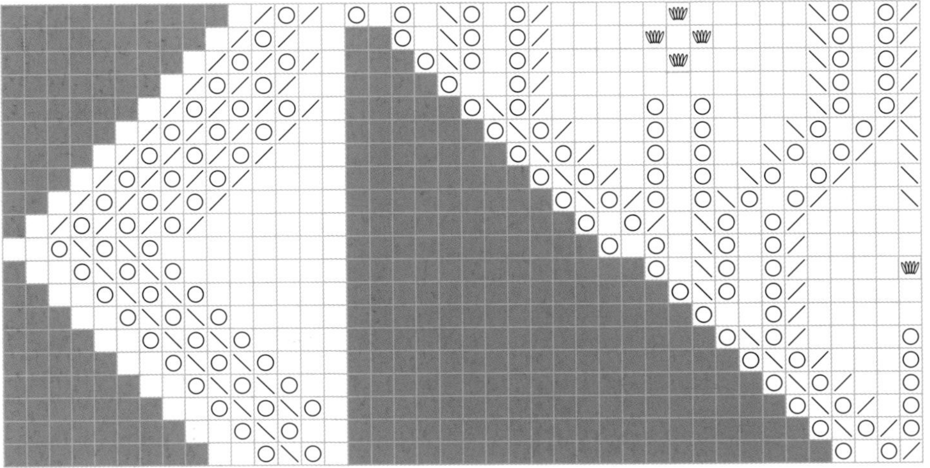

chart continues across page

Only odd-numbered rows are charted;
all even-numbered rows are purl across.

Flutter Shawl Chart 1, continued

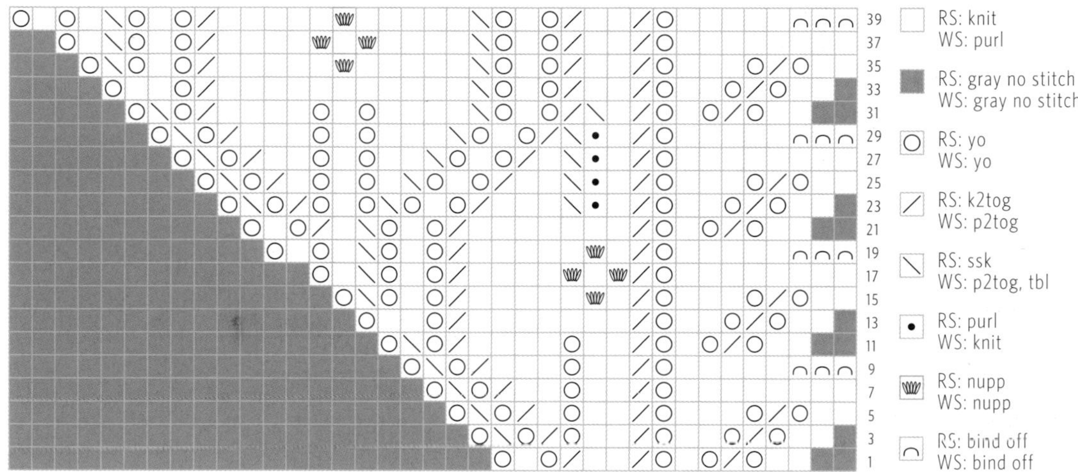

Flutter Shawl Chart 2, continued

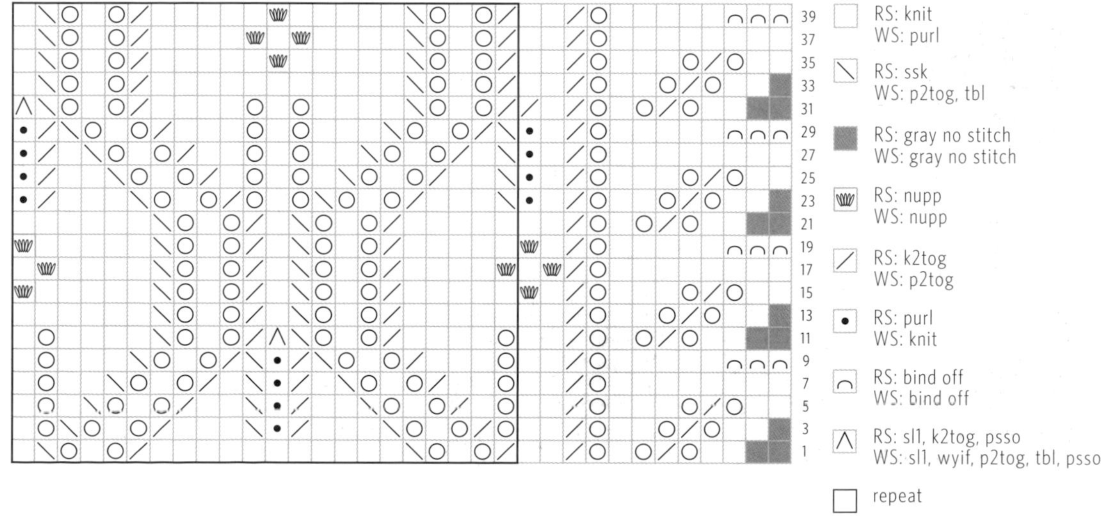

Flutter Shawl Chart 3

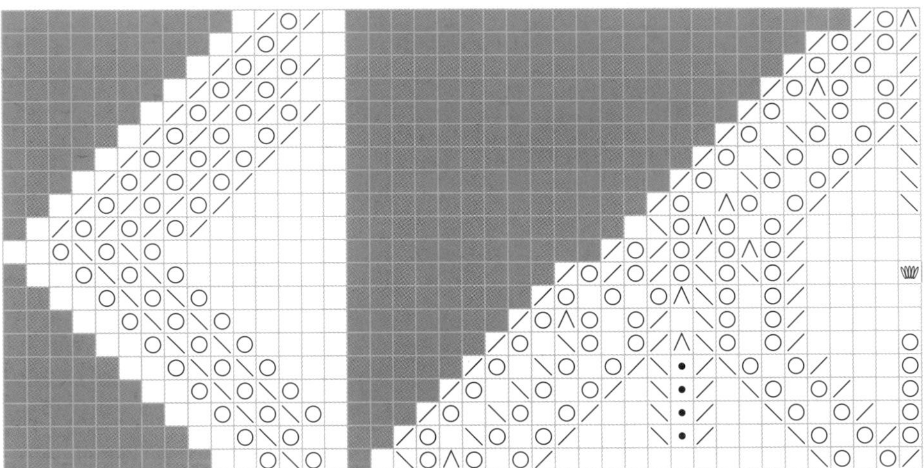

chart continues
across page

Flutter Shawl Chart 3, continued

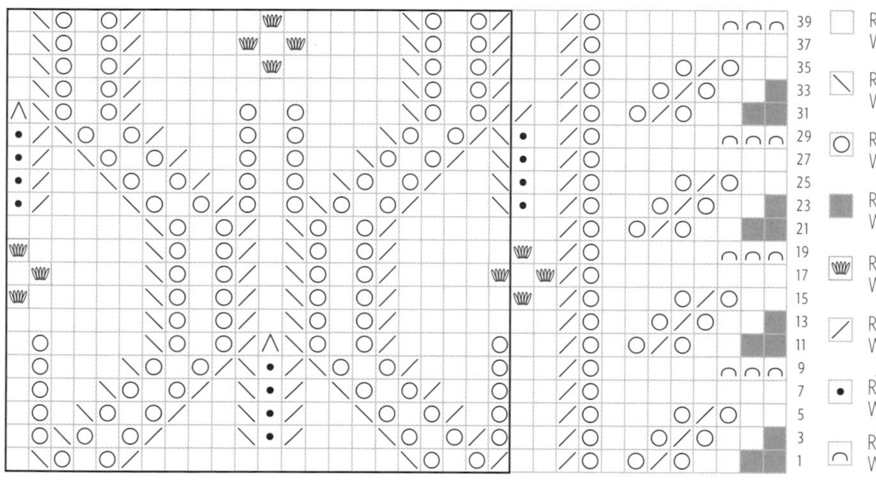

- RS: knit / WS: purl
- RS: ssk / WS: p2tog, tbl
- RS: yo / WS: yo
- RS: gray no stitch / WS: gray no stitch
- RS: nupp / WS: nupp
- RS: k2tog / WS: p2tog
- RS: purl / WS: knit
- RS: bind off / WS: bind off
- RS: sl1, k2tog, psso / WS: sl1, wyif, p2tog, tbl, psso
- repeat

Flutter Shawl Chart 4

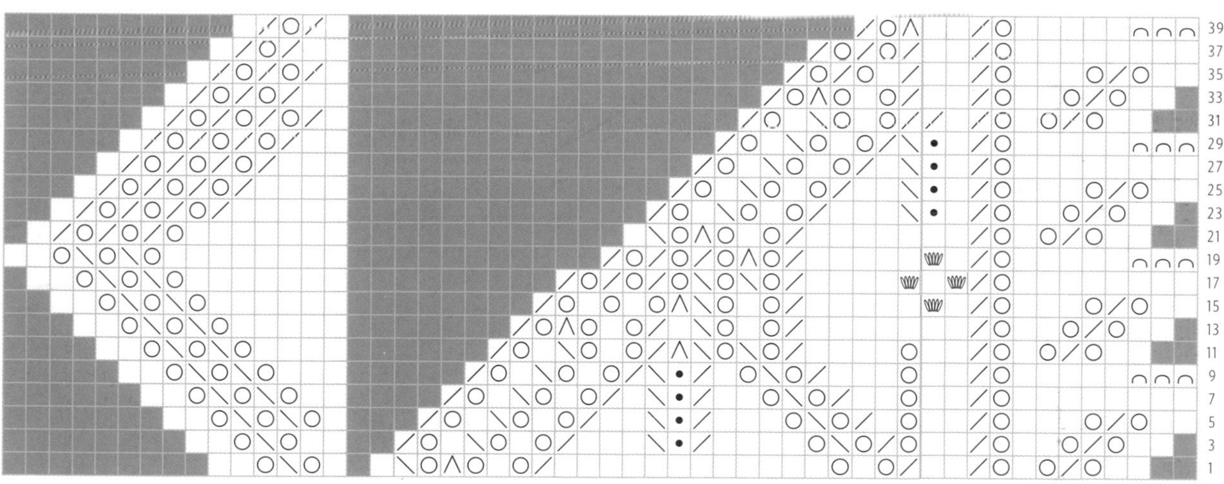

- RS: knit / WS: purl
- RS: gray no stitch / WS: gray no stitch
- RS: yo / WS: yo
- RS: ssk / WS: p2tog, tbl
- RS: k2tog / WS: p2tog
- RS: sl1, k2tog, psso / WS: sl1, wyif, p2tog, tbl, psso
- RS: nupp / WS: nupp
- RS: bind off / WS: bind off
- RS: purl / WS: knit

poppy shawl

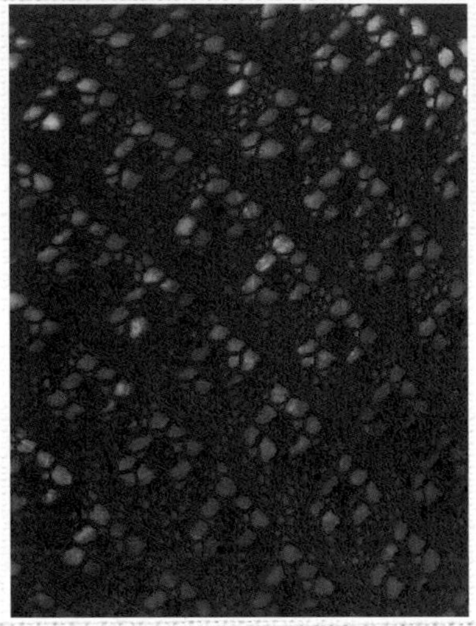

The Triangle Tulip Shawl (page 24) is made using two triangles. Add a third triangle, and you get three-fourths of a square. This shape is so easy to wear! With a square back, it is flattering on most body types. Instead of a single center spine stitch between triangles, I used a wider panel, which allows the shawl to stay squarely on the shoulders.

For this shawl, I chose to use Lopi Einband. A single-ply Icelandic wool, this yarn is available in a multitude of brilliant colors. It is a "sticky" wool, which will give great stitch definition for those center panels. Note that the stitch pattern for the center panels has lace on both sides!

FINISHED MEASUREMENTS

40"/101.5cm wide, measured from one front tip to next corner

43"/109cm long, measured between the two back corners

20"/51cm measured from back neck to lower edge

MATERIALS AND TOOLS

Lopi Einband (100% pure Icelandic wool; 1.75oz/50g = 245yd/224m): 4 skeins, color #9142—approx 800yds/731.5m of sock weight yarn (1)

Knitting needles: 3.5mm (size 4 U.S.) 40" circular needle or size to obtain gauge

Stitch markers

Tapestry needle

GAUGE

17 sts/32 rows of Floral Diamonds Lace pattern = 4"/10cm, washed and blocked

Always take time to check your gauge.

Notes

7-stitch nupps are used throughout.

The Floral Diamonds Lace pattern stitch definition is provided for swatching purposes and does not exactly match row instructions for the shawl itself.

All rows are charted.

PATTERN STITCHES

floral diamonds lace

Worked over a repeat of 8 sts plus 5

Row 1 (RS): K1, yo, (ssk, k6, yo) repeat across to last 4 sts, ssk, k2.

Row 2 and all WS rows: Purl across.

Row 3: K2, (yo, ssk, k3, k2tog, yo, k1) repeat across to last 3 sts, k3.

Row 5: K3, (yo, ssk, k1, k2tog, yo, k3) repeat across to last 2 sts, k2.

Row 7: K1, k2tog, (yo, k5, yo, sk2p) repeat across to last 2 sts, yo, k2.

Row 9: K5, (yo, ssk, k6) repeat across.

Row 11: K3, (k2tog, yo, k1, yo, ssk, k3) repeat across to last 2 sts, k2.

Row 13: K2, (k2tog, yo, k3, yo, ssk, k1) repeat across to last 3 sts, k3.

Row 15: K4, (yo, sk2p, yo, k5) repeat across to last st, k1.

INSTRUCTIONS

tab

Cast on 4 sts.

Starting with WS row, work 65 rows in St st.

Next row: K4, pick up and knit 45 sts in selvedge edge, pick up and knit 4 sts in cast on edge—53 sts.

Turn.

Next row: P4, PM, (p1, PM, p21, PM), repeat 2 times, p1, PM, p4. (You have divided your knitting into 7 sections.)

begin working charts

Row 1: K4, *work across chart 1, then chart 2; repeat from * once more, work chart 1 once more, k4—59 sts.

Continue to work through row 10 of charts 1 and 2, keeping the first and last 4 sts in St st—83 sts.

Row 11: K4, *work across chart 3, then chart 4; repeat from * once more, work chart 3 once, k4—89 sts.

Continue to work through row 16 of charts 3 and 4—131 sts.

Repeat rows 1–16 of charts 3 and 4 eight more times, repeating highlighted section of chart 3 as sts increase, then repeat rows 1–8 once—539 sts.

Bind off loosely.

FINISHING

Weave in all ends.

Block piece to measurements.

All rows are charted.

Poppy Shawl Chart 1

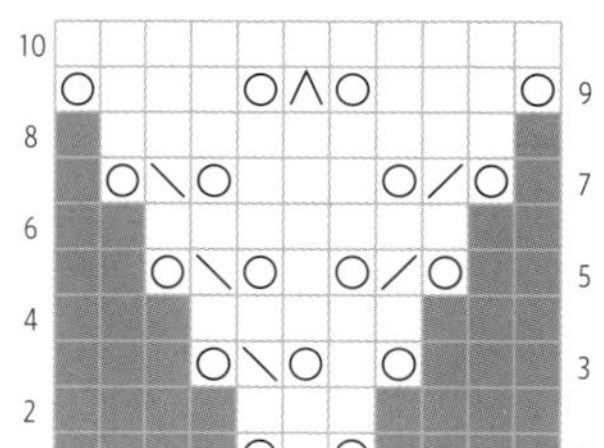

- RS: knit / WS: purl
- RS: yo / WS: yo
- RS: ssk / WS: p2tog, tbl
- RS: k2tog / WS: p2tog
- RS: sl1, k2tog, psso / WS: sl1, wyif, p2tog, tbl, psso
- RS: gray no stitch / WS: gray no stitch

Poppy Shawl Chart 2

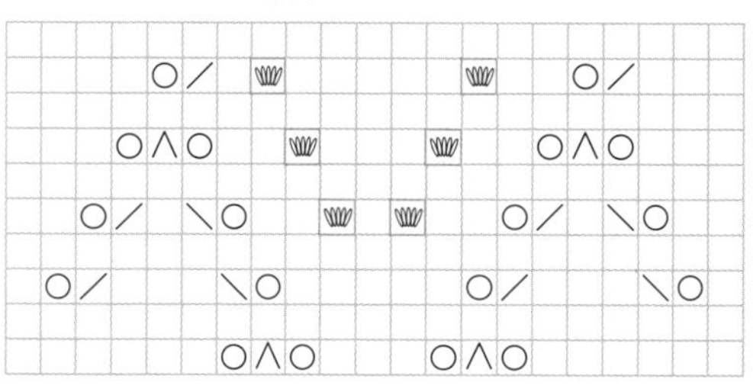

- RS: knit / WS: purl
- RS: yo / WS: yo
- RS: sl1, k2tog, psso / WS: sl1, wyif, p2tog, tbl, psso
- RS: k2tog / WS: p2tog
- RS: ssk / WS: p2tog, tbl
- nupp

Poppy Shawl Chart 3

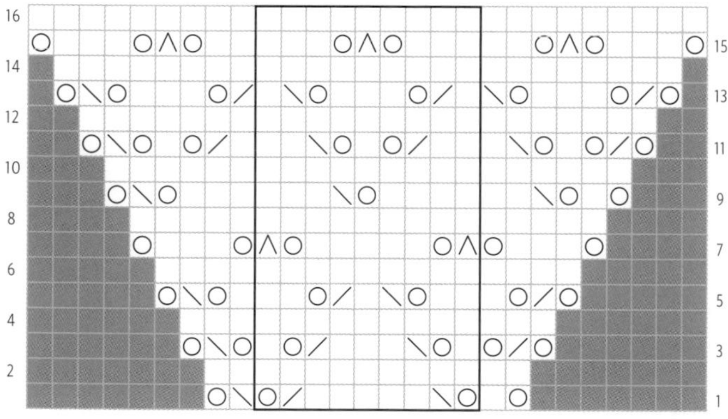

Poppy Shawl Chart 4

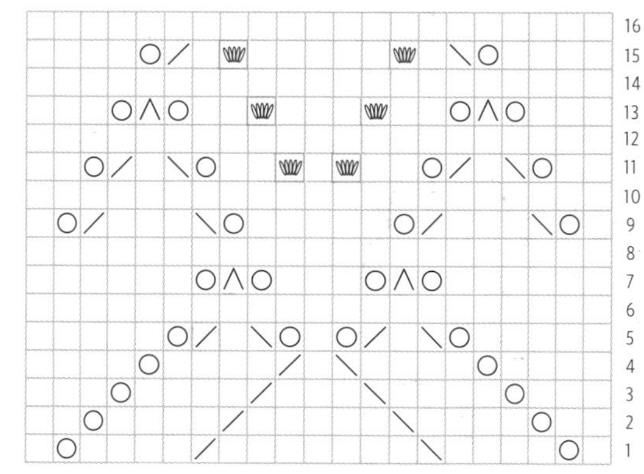

- RS: knit / WS: purl
- RS: yo / WS: yo
- RS: gray no stitch / WS: gray no stich
- RS: ssk / WS: p2tog, tbl
- RS: k2tog / WS: p2tog
- RS: sl1, k2tog, psso / WS: sl1, wyif, p2tog, tbl, psso
- nupp
- repeat

floral tunic

To create a top-down raglan sweater, we increase one stitch every other row on either side of four seam stitches, at the point where the body meets the arms. In essence, then, we are creating four squared-off triangles, one for each of the sleeves and one each for the front and back (see raglan schematic on page 42).

For this design, I wanted to extend the triangle motif and create an A-line tunic. Keeping the raglan shaping lines intact after the sleeves were completed, I continued the increases in the side gusset sections only. This allows the garment to slowly flare, adding fullness over the tummy and hips with a long vertical line, which slims every body type. The drape of the yarn gives movement to the tunic. Make it short, as shown, to wear with jeans, or make a longer version to wear over leggings or a skirt. Either way, this will quickly become a go-to piece in your wardrobe. The simple eight-row lace motif is easy to master, yet has enough depth to keep your interest.

SIZES

Small (Medium, Large)

FINISHED MEASUREMENTS

Bust 44 (48, 52)"/112 (122, 132)cm

MATERIALS AND TOOLS

Fyberspates Scrumptious 4-ply sport superwash (45% silk, 55% superwash merino; 3.5oz/100g = 399yds/365m): 3 (3, 4) skeins, color #308—approx 1050 (1200, 1300)yds/948.5 (1081, 1188m) of sport weight yarn (2)

Knitting needles: 2.75mm (size 2 U.S.) 16" circular, 3.5mm (size 4 U.S.) 16" and 32" circulars, 1 set of 4 or 5 DPNs or size to obtain gauge

Stitch markers

Stitch holders

Tapestry needle

GAUGE

18 sts/22 rows = 4"/10cm over Floral Diamonds pattern, washed and blocked

Always take time to check your gauge.

Notes

5-stitch nupps are used throughout.

The Floral Diamonds pattern stitch definition is provided for swatching purposes and does not exactly match row instructions for the tunic itself.

Only odd-numbered rounds are charted; all even-numbered rounds are knit around.

Tunic is worked from the neck down.

PATTERN STITCHES

floral diamonds

Worked over a repeat of 8 sts + 4

Row 1: K2, (yo, ssk, k3, k2tog, yo, k1) repeat across, end k2.

Row 2 and all WS rows: Purl across, completing nupps as needed when you come to them.

Row 3: K2, (k1, yo, ssk, k1, k2tog, yo, k1, make nupp) repeat across, end k2.

Row 5: K2, (k2tog, yo, k3, yo, ssk, k1) repeat across, end k2.

Row 7: Yo, sk2p, (yo, k5, yo, sk2p) repeat across, end yo, k1.

Row 9: K2, (k1, k2tog, yo, k1, yo, ssk, k2) repeat across, end k2.

Row 11: K2, (k2tog, yo, k1, make nupp, k1, yo, ssk, k1) repeat across, end k2.

Row 13: K2, (k1, yo, ssk, k1, k2tog, yo, k2) repeat across, end k2.

Row 15: K2, (k2, yo, sk2p, yo, k3) repeat across, end k2.

INSTRUCTIONS

With 2.75mm (size 2 U.S.) 16" needle, cast on 96 (104, 112) sts.

neckband

Join to work in the round, being careful not to twist sts. Place marker for beginning of round.

Rounds 1–5: (K2, p2) repeat around.

In next round, use markers of different color from beginning of round marker.

Round 6: *K40 (42, 44), PM, k8 (10, 12), PM; repeat from * once more using beginning of round marker for last marker.

Begin Raglan Shaping

Switch to larger needle.

Size Small

Round 7: *K1, yo, knit to marker, yo, slip marker; repeat from * around—104 sts.

Round 8 and all even rounds to end: Knit around.

Size Medium

Round 7: Knit around, slipping markers when you come to them.

Round 8 and all even rounds to end: Knit around.

Size Large

Round 7: *K1, yo, knit to marker, yo, slip marker; repeat from * around—120 sts.

Round 8 and all even rounds to end: Knit around.

Rounds 9 and 11: Repeat round 7—136 sts.

All Sizes

Begin working charts between markers:

Repeat chart 1 rows 1–8 5 (6, 6) times, then repeat chart rows 1–7 once—296 (328, 360) sts total: 89 (97, 105) front and back sts, 57 (65, 73) sleeve sts, 4 seam sts.

divide for sleeves and body

Next round: *Knit to marker, remove marker, k1, slip the next 57 (65, 73) sts to holder for sleeve, slip marker, cast on 9 sts for underarm, place marker, repeat from * once more—200 (216, 232) sts rem for body.

body

Working on 200 (216, 232) body sts, begin working charts 2 and 3, increasing 4 sts every odd round in underarm gussets as follows:

*Work chart 2 to marker, slip marker, work chart 3 to marker, slip marker; repeat from * once more.

Repeat charts 2 and 3 rows 1–16 eight times, or until tunic is desired length. Bind off loosely knitwise.

sleeves

With RS facing, using 16" needle or DPNs (for size Small), begin at center of underarm and cast on sts. Pick up and knit 4 sts, knit across 57 (65, 73) held sleeve sts, pick up and knit 5 sts in underarm, place marker for beginning of round—66, 74, 82 sts total. Join to work in the round.

Change to DPNs when number of sts has been sufficiently decreased.

Repeat chart 4 rows 1–24 until 30 (36, 38) sts remain, decreasing 1 st each end every 6th round as charted, or until sleeve is desired length, ending with row 8, 16, or 24.

Bind off loosely knitwise.

FINISHING

Weave in all ends.

Block piece to measurements.

Raglan Schematic

10 (11½, 11½)" / 25.4 (29.2, 29.2)cm

44 (48, 52)" / 111.8 (122, 132)cm

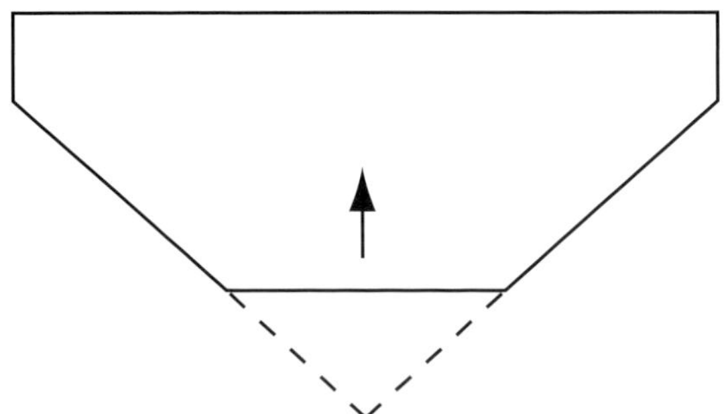

Floral Tunic Chart 1

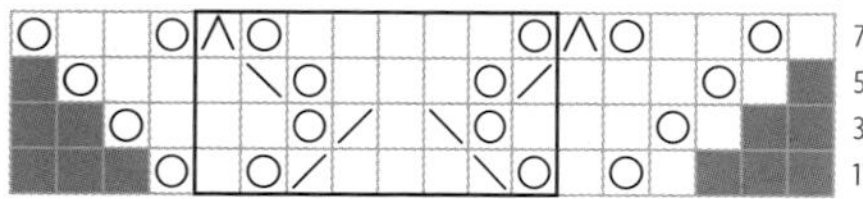

- RS: knit / WS: purl
- RS: yo / WS: yo
- RS: gray no stitch / WS: gray no stitch
- RS: sl1, k2tog, psso / WS: sl1, wyif, p2tog, tbl, psso
- RS: k2tog / WS: p2tog
- RS: ssk / WS: p2tog, tbl
- repeat

Floral Tunic Chart 2

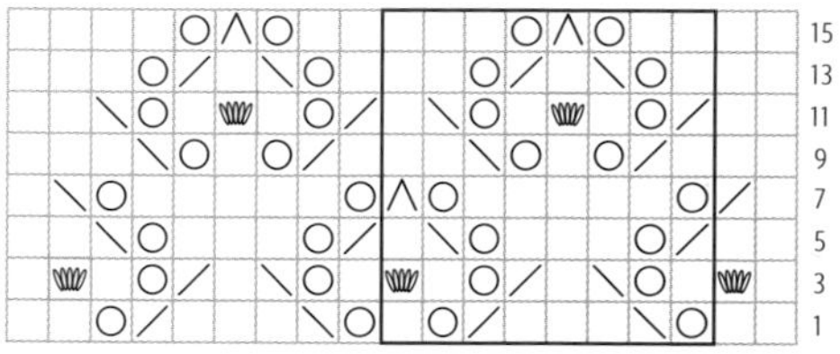

15
13
11
9
7
5
3
1

- RS: knit / WS: purl
- RS: yo / WS: yo
- RS: sl1, k2tog, psso / WS: sl1, wyif, p2tog, tbl, psso
- RS: k2tog / WS: p2tog
- RS: ssk / WS: p2tog, tbl
- RS: nupp / WS: nupp
- repeat

Only odd-numbered rounds are charted; all even-numbered rounds are knit around.

Floral Tunic Chart 3

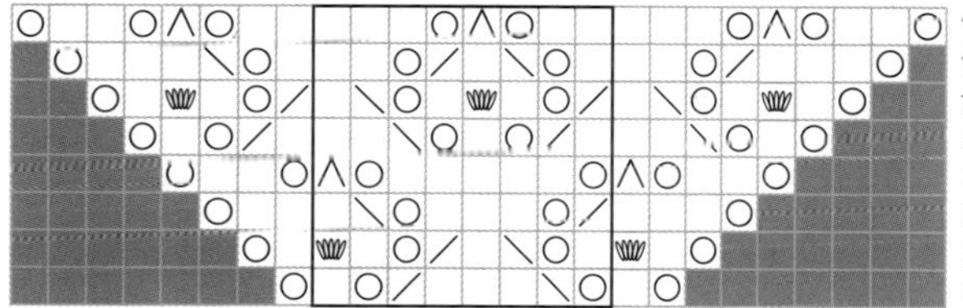

- RS: knit / WS: purl
- RS: yo / WS: yo
- RS: sl1, k2tog, psso / WS: sl1, wyif, p2tog, tbl, psso
- RS: k2tog / WS: p2tog
- RS: ssk / WS: p2tog, tbl
- RS: nupp / WS: nupp
- RS: gray no stitch / WS: gray no stitch
- repeat

Floral Tunic Chart 4

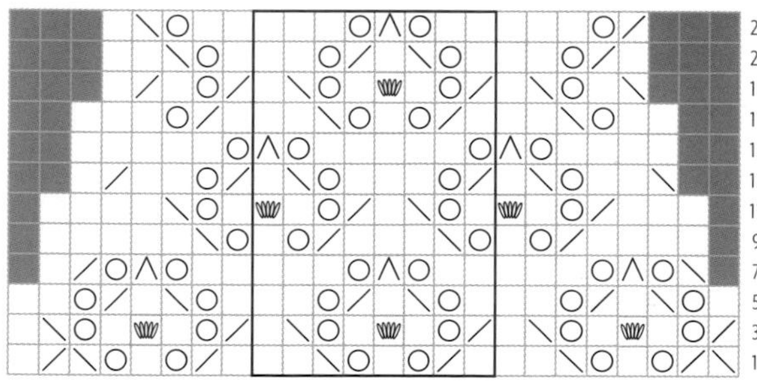

- RS: knit / WS: purl
- RS: yo / WS: yo
- RS: k2tog / WS: p2tog
- RS: ssk / WS: p2tog, tbl
- RS: sl1, k2tog, psso / WS: sl1, wyif, p2tog, tbl, psso
- RS: gray no stitch / WS: gray no stitch
- RS: nupp / WS: nupp
- repeat

rectangles

THE SIMPLE RECTANGLE IS the easiest of shapes to work with in lace design, with no shaping required! Just pick a favorite lace motif, cast on either the width or the length, and knit away. Any size rectangle can be adapted to some type of accessory or garment, be it a scarf, a stole, or even a vest. In this chapter, I give you a few ideas for projects to use as a jumping-off point for your own exploration. Try cutting an 18 x 60-inch (45.7 x 152.4 cm) rectangle of knit stretch fabric. Drape it around a dress form and see what types of pieces you can develop. You'll be amazed at the variety of options!

japanese leaf scarf

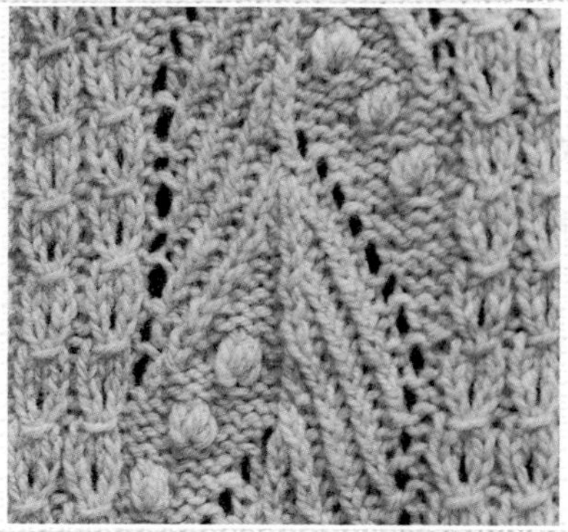

A SCARF IS THE OBVIOUS STARTING POINT for any exploration of rectangles. An important factor in any scarf design is its reversibility. The "wrong" side of a scarf may be visible, so it's important to make sure it's just as attractive as the right side! For that reason, I chose this Japanese Leaf motif. The combination of reverse stockinette and twisted rib stitches ensures that both sides of the fabric will be appealing. I chose Tibetan Dream yarn for this project because it is luxuriously soft, which is a must for any scarf, yet also has great stitch definition, which makes those twisted stitches and mock cables pop! To learn how to turn this scarf into a beautiful stole, turn to page 50!

FINISHED MEASUREMENTS

6½ x 65"/16.5 x 165cm

MATERIALS AND TOOLS

Bijou Spun Tibetan Dream (85% yak down, 15% nylon; 4oz/113g = 440yds/402m): 1 skein, color #12—approx 440yds/402m of sock weight yarn (1)

Knitting needles: 3.75mm (size 5 U.S.) or size to obtain gauge

Stitch markers

Tapestry needle

GAUGE

1 repeat of chart 1 (18 sts/30 rows) = 3½"/9cm square

Always take time to check your gauge.

Notes

7-stitch nupps are used throughout. On return rows, complete nupps by working p7tog.

All rows are charted.

Special Abbreviations

Mock Cable (worked over 3 sts): Slip the 3rd st on left-hand needle over the first 2 sts and off needles. Into the remaining 2 sts work k1, yo, k1 (3 sts made out of 3 sts).

PATTERN STITCHES

japanese leaf (chart 1)

Row 1 (RS): P1, yo, ssk, p6, ssk, (ktbl, p1) 3 times, yo, p1.

Row 2: K3, (ptbl, k1) 2 times, ptbl, p1, k6, p1, k2.

Row 3: P1, yo, p1, ssk, p2, make nupp, p2, ssk, p1, (ktbl, p1) 2 times, yo, p2.

Row 4: K4, (ptbl, k1) 2 times, p1, k2, complete nupp, k2, (p1, k1) 2 times.

Row 5: P1, yo, ktbl, p1, ssk, p4, ssk, (ktbl, p1) 2 times, yo, p3.

Row 6: K5, ptbl, k1, ptbl, p1, k4, p1, k1, ptbl, k2.

Row 7: P1, yo, p1, ktbl, p1, ssk, p3, ssk, p1, ktbl, p1, yo, p4.

Row 8: K6, ptbl, k1, p1, k3, p1, k1, ptbl, k1, p1, k1.

Row 9: P1, yo, (ktbl, p1) 2 times, ssk, p2, ssk, ktbl, p1, yo, p3, make nupp, p1.

Row 10: K1, complete nupp, k5, ptbl, p1, k2, p1, (k1, ptbl) 2 times, k2.

Row 11: P1, yo, p1, (ktbl, p1) 2 times, (ssk, p1) 2 times, yo, p6.

Row 12: K8, (p1, k1) 2 times, (ptbl, k1) 2 times, p1, k1.

Row 13: P1, yo, (ktbl, p1) 3 times, ssk, ssk, yo, p3, make nupp, p3.

Row 14: K3, complete nupp, k4, p2, (k1, ptbl) 3 times, k2.

Row 15: P1, yo, (p1, ktbl) 3 times, p1, ssk, p6, k2tog, yo.

Row 16: K1, p1, k6, p1, (k1, ptbl) 3 times, k3.

Row 17: P2, yo, (p1, ktbl) 3 times, k2tog, p2, make nupp, p2, k2tog, p1, yo.

Row 18: P1, k1, p1, k2, complete nupp, k2, p1, (ptbl, k1) 3 times, k3.

Row 19: P3, yo, (p1, ktbl) 2 times, p1, k2tog, p4, k2tog, p1, ktbl, yo.

Row 20: K1, ptbl, k1, p1, k4, p1, k1, (ptbl, k1) 2 times, k4.

Row 21: P4, yo, (p1, ktbl) 2 times, k2tog, p3, k2tog, p1, ktbl, p1, yo.

Row 22: P1, k1, ptbl, k1, p1, k3, p1, (ptbl, k1) 2 times, k5.

Row 23: P5, yo, p1, ktbl, p1, k2tog, p2, k2tog, (p1, ktbl) 2 times, yo.

Row 24: (K1, ptbl) 2 times, k1, p1, k2, p1, k1, ptbl, k7.

Row 25: P2, make nupp, p3, yo, p1, ktbl, k2tog, p1, k2tog, p1, (ktbl, p1) 2 times, yo.

Row 26: P1, (k1, ptbl) 2 times, (k1, p1) 2 times, ptbl, p5, complete nupp, p2.

Row 27: P7, yo, p1, k2tog, k2tog, (p1, ktbl) 3 times, yo.

Row 28: (K1, ptbl) 3 times, k1, p2, k9.

Row 29: P4, make nupp, p3, yo, k3tog, (p1, ktbl) 3 times, p1, yo.

Row 30: K2, (ptbl, k1) 3 times, p1, k4, complete nupp, k4.

mock cable (chart 2)

Row 1 (RS): P1, k3.

Row 2: P3, k1.

Row 3: P1, mock cable.

Row 4: Repeat row 2.

INSTRUCTIONS

Cast on 39 sts.

Set-up row (WS): P2, k1, PM, (p3, k1, PM) 2 times, k2, (p1, k1) 4 times, k8, PM, (p3, k1, PM) 2 times p2.

Begin Lace Pattern

Row 1 and all RS rows: K2, work chart 2 (Mock Cable) twice, work chart 1 (Japanese Leaf) once, work chart 2 (Mock Cable) twice, end p1, k2.

Row 2 and all WS rows: P2, k1, work chart 2 twice, work chart 1 once, work chart 2 twice, end p2.

Work even in pattern as established until 14 repeats of chart 1 have been worked, or until scarf is desired length. Bind off loosely in pattern.

Finishing

Weave in all ends.

Block piece to measurements.

Japanese Leaf Scarf and Cables and Lace Stole

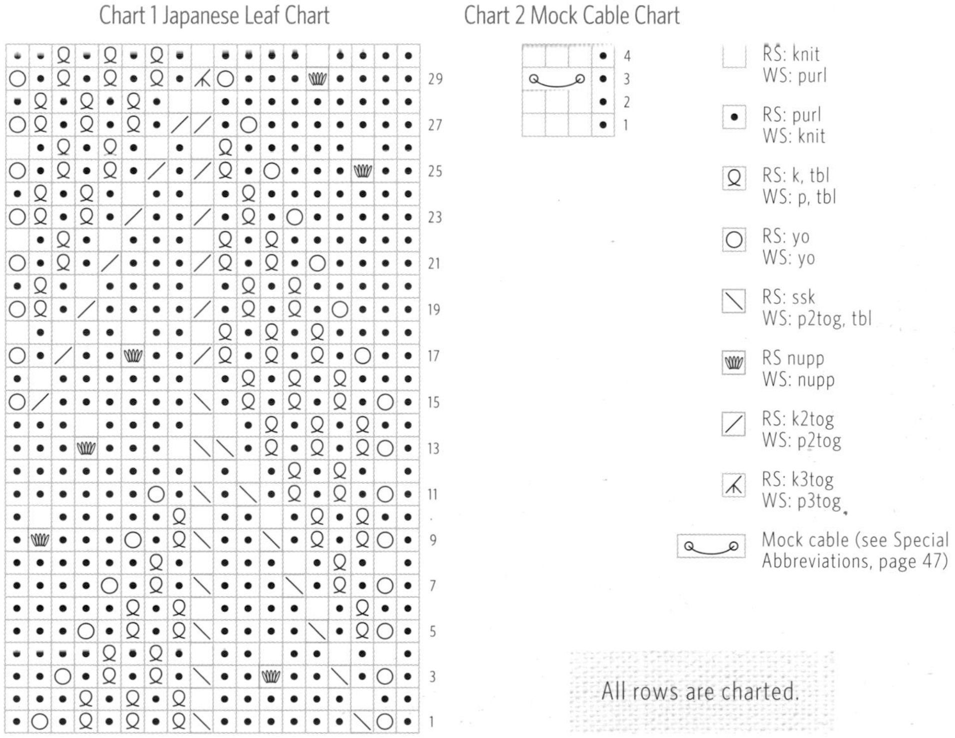
Chart 1 Japanese Leaf Chart
Chart 2 Mock Cable Chart
RS: knit
WS: purl
RS: purl
WS: knit
RS: k, tbl
WS: p, tbl
RS: yo
WS: yo
RS: ssk
WS: p2tog, tbl
RS nupp
WS: nupp
RS: k2tog
WS: p2tog
RS: k3tog
WS: p3tog
Mock cable (see Special Abbreviations, page 47)

All rows are charted.

VARIATION

cables and lace stole

EXPAND A SCARF AND KNIT IT LENGTHWISE, and now you have a stole. But this piece, a variation of the Japanese Leaf Scarf on page 46, is more than just a stole. Snaps placed along the edges allow you to manipulate and drape it into a variety of garments. You can make an infinity scarf, a cowl, or even a vest. I used Lopi Einband, a lace weight Icelandic wool. These wools have stitch definition that is incomparable, and the color range is amazing. I also chose to double the yarn. Initially, my decision was practical; with such a large piece, I wanted to give the knitter the option of using larger needles! However, after swatching, I was excited by how the yarn knit up when doubled. The two strands don't blend into one, as usually happens when yarn is doubled. Instead, because of the structure of the Einband, the strands stay separate, which lends a unique depth and dimension to the knitting.

FINISHED MEASUREMENTS

17 x 62"/43 x 157.5cm

MATERIALS AND TOOLS

Lopi Einband (100% pure Icelandic wool; 1.75 oz/50g = 245yds/224m): 4 balls, color crimson #0047—approx 245yds/224m of sock weight yarn (1)

Knitting needles: 4.5mm (size 7 U.S.) 40" circular or size to obtain gauge

Stitch markers

Tapestry needle

9 sew-on snaps

Sewing needle and thread

GAUGE

1 repeat of chart 1 (18 sts/30 rows) = 5"/12.5cm wide x 6"/15cm tall with yarn held doubled, washed and blocked

Always take time to check your gauge.

Charts can be found on page 49.

INSTRUCTIONS

With yarn held doubled, cast on 235 sts.

SET-UP ROW: P2, k1, p2, k1, pm, p3, k1, pm, *k2, (p1, k1) 4 times, k8, pm, p3, k1, pm *; repeat from * to * across, end p2, k1, p2.

Begin Lace Pattern

ROW 1 AND ALL RS ROWS: K2, p1, k2, *work chart 2 between markers, work chart 1 between markers*; repeat from * to * across, end work chart 2 between markers, p1, k2, p1, k2.

ROW 2 AND ALL WS ROWS: P2, k1, p2, k1, *work chart 2 between markers, work chart 1 between markers*; repeat from * to * across, end work chart 2 between markers, p2, k1, p2.

Work in pattern as established, repeating charts 1 and 2 between markers, until 3 repeats of chart 1 have been completed. Bind off loosely in pattern.

FINISHING

Block piece to measurements. Weave in all ends.

With sewing thread, sew snaps along selvedge edge, placing male snaps along left edge evenly spaced and female snaps along right edge opposite male snaps.

lopi yarns

Lopi yarns are imported from Iceland, and the history of these yarns is incredibly fascinating. The wool comes from the Icelandic sheep, which has two distinct fibers—a long, glossy, and tough outer fiber, and a fine, soft, and insulating inner fiber. The yarns look like unspun singles, but are actually two strands of these fibers lightly twisted together. The result is a fabric that is incredibly light, yet insulating. Lopi may be a little rough to the hand (a quick soak in a hair conditioner solution softens it incredibly—see instructions on page 25); however, it yields a fabric that will last a lifetime with no pilling or wear.

butterfly stole

Take two rectangles and put them together, and you get a beautiful "L" shape. This is a wonderfully wearable accessory, perfect for the chill of a restaurant in the summer or as a snuggly stole over a coat in the winter. The shape lends itself to a variety of options for draping around the neck or shoulders. For this piece, I chose to use one of my favorite luxury yarn combinations. Filatura Di Crosa Superior is a lace weight cashmere that is brushed to produce a halo. Held together with Nirvana, a lace weight merino wool, the resulting fabric is light as a feather, yet it has body. A combination of knits and purls, with a few cables thrown in for good measure, creates this butterfly motif, which looks pretty on both sides of the fabric.

FINISHED MEASUREMENTS

13"/33cm wide at each end
36"/91.5cm long measured across one long edge

MATERIALS AND TOOLS

Filatura Di Crosa Superior (70% cashmere, 25% silk, 5% extrafine merino; 0.88oz/25g = 328yds/300m): (A), 4 balls, color #65—approx 2100yds/1920m of lace weight yarn (0)

Filatura Di Crosa Nirvana (100% extrafine merino wool; 0.88oz/25g = 372yds/340m): (B), 4 balls, color #48—approx 2100yds/1920m of lace weight yarn (0)

Knitting needles: 3.75mm (size 5 U.S.) or size to obtain gauge

Cable needles

Tapestry needle

GAUGE

32 sts/34 rows = 4"/10cm over stitch pattern, with 1 strand each of A and B held together, washed and blocked

Always take time to check your gauge.

Note

All rows are charted.

Special Abbreviations

2-2-2 LPC: Slip 2 sts to cable needle and hold in front. Slip the next 2 sts to 2nd cable needle and hold in back. Knit 2 from left-hand needle, p2 from back cable needle, k2 from front cable needle.

2-2-2 RPC: Slip 4 sts to cable needle and hold in back. Knit 2 from left-hand needle. Slip the last 2 (purl) sts from cable needle back to left-hand needle and p2. Knit 2 from cable needle.

PATTERN STITCHES

butterflies lace

Row 1 (RS): K5, (p1, k2tog, yo, k1, p2, k1, yo, ssk, p1, k4) repeat across to last st, k1.

Row 2: P1, (p4, k1, p3, k2, p3, k1) repeat across to last 5 sts, p5

Row 3: K4, (p1, k2tog, yo, k2, p2, k2, yo, ssk, p1, k2) repeat across to last 2 sts, k2.

Row 4: P2, (p2, k1, p4, k2, p4, k1) repeat across to last 4 sts, p4.

Row 5: K2, (p2, k2tog, yo, k3, p2, k3, yo, ssk) repeat across to last 4 sts, p2, k2.

Row 6: P2, (k2, p5) repeat across to last 4 sts, k2, p2.

Row 7: K2, p2, (k3, k2tog, yo, p2, yo, ssk, k3, p2) repeat across to last 2 sts, k2.

Row 8: P2, (k2, p4, k4, p4) repeat across to last 4 sts, k2, p2.

Row 9: K2, p2, (k2, k2tog, yo, p1, k2, p1, yo, ssk, k2, p2) repeat across to last 2 sts, k2.

Row 10: P2, (k2, p3, k2, p2, k2, p3) repeat across to last 4 sts, k2, p2.

Row 11: K2, p2, (k1, k2tog, yo, p1, k4, p1, yo, ssk, k1, p2) repeat across to last 2 sts, k2.

Row 12: P2, (k2, p2, k2, p4, k2, p2), repeat across to last 4 sts, k2, p2.

Row 13: K2, p2, k2, (p1, k6, p1, 2-2-2 RPC) repeat across to last 14 sts, p1, k6, p1, k2, p2, k2.

Row 14: P2, (k2, p2, k1, p6, k1, p2) repeat across to last 4 sts, k2, p2.

Row 15: K2, p2, (k1, yo, ssk, p1, k4, p1, k2tog, yo, k1, p2) repeat across to last 2 sts, k2.

Row 16: P2, (k2, p3, k1, p4, k1, p3) repeat across to last 4 sts, k2, p2.

Row 17: K2, p2, (k2, yo, ssk, p1, k2, p1, k2tog, yo, k2, p2) repeat across to last 2 sts, k2.

Row 18: P2, (k2, p4, k1, p2, k1, p4) repeat across to last 4 sts, k2, p2.

Row 19: K2, p2, (k3, yo, ssk, p2, k2tog, yo, k3, p2) repeat across to last 2 sts, k2.

Row 20: P2, (k2, p5) repeat across to last 4 sts, k2, p2.

Row 21: K2, p2, (yo, ssk, k3, p2, k3, k2tog, yo, p2) repeat across to last 2 sts, k2.

Row 22: P2, k3, (p4, k2, p4, k4) repeat across to last 15 sts, p4, k2, p4, k3, p2.

Row 23: K4, (p1, yo, ssk, k2, p2, k2, k2tog, yo, p1, k2) repeat across to last 2 sts, k2.

Row 24: P4, (k2, p3, k2, p3, k2, p2) repeat across to last 2 sts, k2.

Row 25: K5, (p1, yo, ssk, k1, p2, k1, k2tog, yo, p1, k4) repeat across to last st, k1.

Row 26: P5, (k2, p2, k2, p2, k2, p4) repeat across to last st, p1.

Row 27: K6, (p1, 2-2-2 LPC, p1, k6) repeat across.

Row 28: P6, (k1, p2, k2, p2, k1, p6) repeat across.

INSTRUCTIONS

With 3.75mm (size 5 U.S.) needles, and holding both strands of yarn together, cast on 104 sts.

Work chart, or written Butterflies Lace pattern instructions on page 53, repeating highlighted section of chart 6 times across row.

Work rows 1–28 of chart or written instructions 12 times.

Bind off loosely knitwise on RS row. Do not fasten off last stitch, do not break yarn.

With RS facing, turn piece 90° to the right. Pick up and knit 103 sts in selvedge edge—104 sts.

Turn. Begin working chart (or written instructions) over 104 sts, starting with row 28, then repeating rows 1–28 seven times.

Bind off loosely knitwise.

FINISHING

Weave in all ends.

Block piece to measurements.

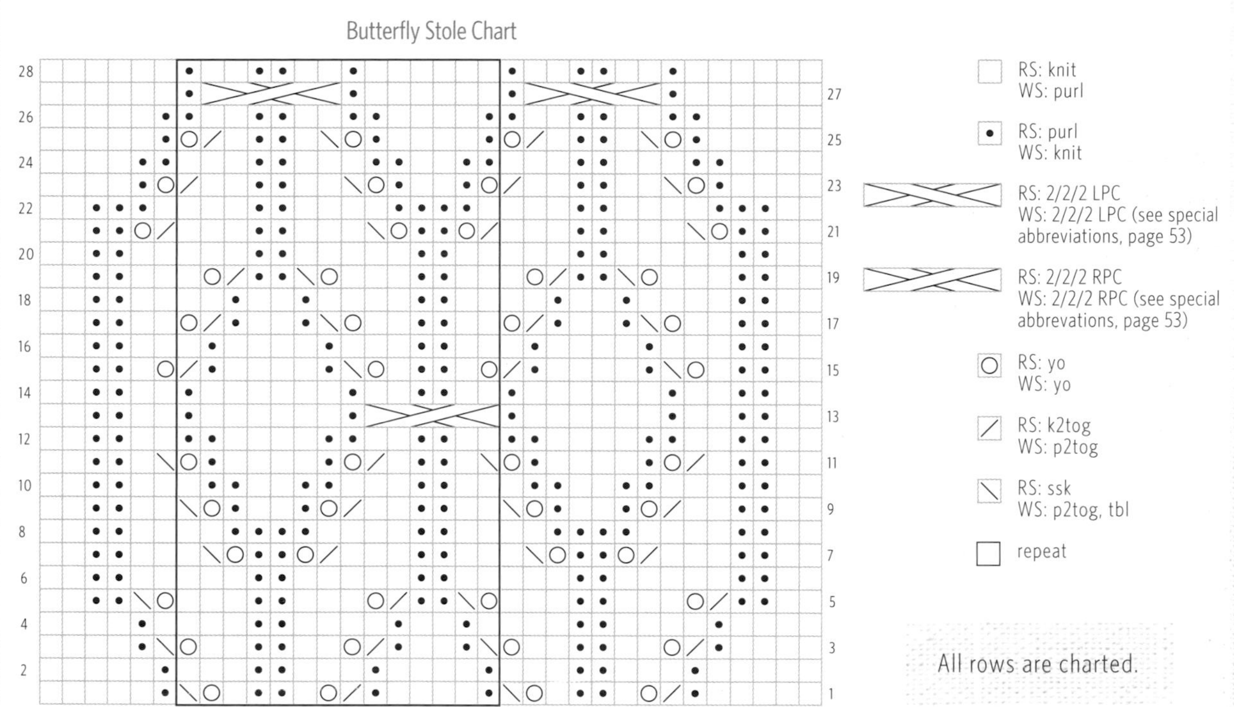
Butterfly Stole Chart
28
26
24
22
20
18
16
14
12
10
8
6
4
2
27
25
23
21
19
17
15
13
11
9
7
5
3
1
RS: knit
WS: purl
RS: purl
WS: knit
RS: 2/2/2 LPC
WS: 2/2/2 LPC (see special abbreviations, page 53)
RS: 2/2/2 RPC
WS: 2/2/2 RPC (see special abbrevations, page 53)
RS: yo
WS: yo
RS: k2tog
WS: p2tog
RS: ssk
WS: p2tog, tbl
repeat
All rows are charted.

posies wrap

This simple wrap is the perfect social knitting project. It's a big rectangle, with armholes created by casting on and then binding off stitches, and its simplicity is the key to its form. The end result is a vest that can be worn long or short, with asymmetrical fronts—a piece that you will throw on again and again. The beauty of this yarn needed to shine, so the lace is simple, with lots of stockinette stitch to show off the tweed. The lace pattern is an Estonian motif, featuring the cross stitches also used in the Starry Nights Bolero on page 60.

SIZES

Small (Medium, Large)

FINISHED MEASUREMENTS

Length 26"/66cm
Width 38 (41, 44)"/96.5 (104, 112)cm

MATERIALS AND TOOLS

Knit One, Crochet Too Elfin Tweed (60% merino wool, 20% baby llama, 10% bamboo, 10% donegal; 1.75oz/50g = 208yds/191m): 6 skeins, color #1392—approx 1200yds/1100m of sock weight yarn (1)

Knitting needles: 3.25mm (size 3 U.S.) or size to obtain gauge

Crochet hook: 3.25mm (size D/3 U.S.)

Stitch markers

Tapestry needle

GAUGE

28 sts/38 rows = 4"/10cm over St st, washed and blocked
Always take time to check your gauge.

Special Abbreviations

2/2: Into the next 2 sts, work k2tog, *do not drop st off left needle,* knit the same 2 sts together through the back loop, drop sts off left needle (2 sts made using 2 sts).

Note

Only odd-numbered rows are charted; all even rows are purl across.

PATTERN STITCHES

estonian heart motif

Row 1: K4, slip marker, *k7, k3tog, yo, k1, yo, 2/2, yo, k1, yo, sk2p, k8, slip marker, repeat from * across, end p4.

Row 2 and all WS rows: Purl across.

Row 3: K4, slip marker, *k6, k3tog, yo, k1, yo, (2/2) 2 times, yo, k1, yo, sk2p, k7, repeat from * across, end k4.

Row 5: K4, slip marker, *k5, k3tog, yo, k1, yo, (2/2) 3 times, yo, k1, yo, sk2p, k6, repeat from * across, end k4.

Row 7: K4, slip marker, *k4, k3tog, yo, k1, yo, (2/2) 4 times, yo, k1, yo, sk2p, k5, repeat from * across, end k4.

Row 9: K4, slip marker, *k3, k3tog, yo, k1, yo, (2/2) 5 times, yo, k1, yo, sk2p, k4, repeat from * across, end k4.

Row 11: K4, slip marker, *k2, k3tog, yo, k1, yo, (2/2) 6 times, yo, k1, yo, sk2p, k3, repeat from * across, end k4.

Row 13: K4, slip marker, *k4, yo, sk2p, yo, (2/2) 2 times, k2, (2/2) 2 times, yo, k3tog, yo, k5, repeat from * across, end k4.

Row 15: K4, *k5, yo, sk2p, yo, 2/2, k4, 2/2, yo, k3tog, yo, k6, repeat from * across, end k4.

Row 17: K4, *k6, yo, sk2p, yo, k6, yo, k3tog, yo, k7, repeat from * across, end k4.

INSTRUCTIONS

right front edge

Cast on 183 sts.

Beginning with RS row, work 3 rows in St st.

Next row: P4, PM, (p25, PM) 7 times, p4.

Keeping the first and last 4 sts in St st, work chart rows 1–17, or written Estonian Heart Motif instructions on page 57, across center 175 sts, repeating chart 7 times across row.

Row 18: P4, slip marker, p25, slip marker, p125, removing markers when you come to them, slip marker, p25, slip marker, p4.

Rows 19–36: Work St st over first 4 sts, work chart rows 1–17 then work row 18 above over next 25 sts, work St st over center 125 sts, work chart rows 1–17 then row 18 above over next 25 sts, work St st over last 4 sts.

Repeat rows 19–36 until piece measures approx 16 (17, 18)"/40.5 (43, 45.5)cm from cast on, ending with a WS row.

armhole opening

Next row (RS): Work in pattern as established across 29 sts, slip marker, k6, bind off next 60 sts, k59, work in pattern as established to end of row.

Next row (WS): P88, cast on 60 sts, p to end of row.

Work in pattern as established until piece measures 30 (32, 34)"/76 (81.5, 86.5)cm from cast on, ending with a WS row. Repeat armhole opening rows.

Continue in pattern as established until piece measures approximately 38 (41, 44)"/96.5 (104, 112)cm from cast on, ending with row 17 of chart.

left front edge

Next row: P4, slip marker, p25, slip marker, (p25, PM) 4 times, p25, slip marker, p25, slip marker, p4.

Work as for right front edge, keeping first and last 4 sts in St st, repeating chart 7 times across row between markers.

Work chart rows 1–17, then work row 18 as instructed in right front edge. Work 4 rows St st. Bind off loosely.

FINISHING

With 3.25mm (size D/3 U.S.) crochet hook, and RS facing, join yarn to right front edge and work 1 row sc around entire piece. Break yarn. Join yarn at underarm and work 1 round sc around armhole opening. Repeat for other opening.

Weave in all ends.

Block piece to measurements.

Posies Wrap Chart

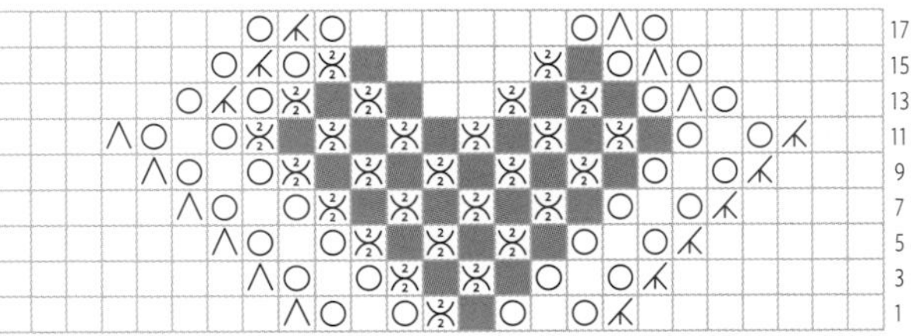

RS: knit
WS: purl

RS: k3tog
WS: p3tog

RS: yo
WS: yo

RS: sl1, k2tog, psso
WS: sl1, wyif, p2tog, tbl, psso

RS: 2 into 2 gathered tbl
WS: 2 into 2 gathered tbl
(see Special Abbreviations, page 57)

RS: gray no stitch
WS: gray no stitch

Only odd-numbered rows are charted; all even-numbered rows are purl across.

starry nights bolero

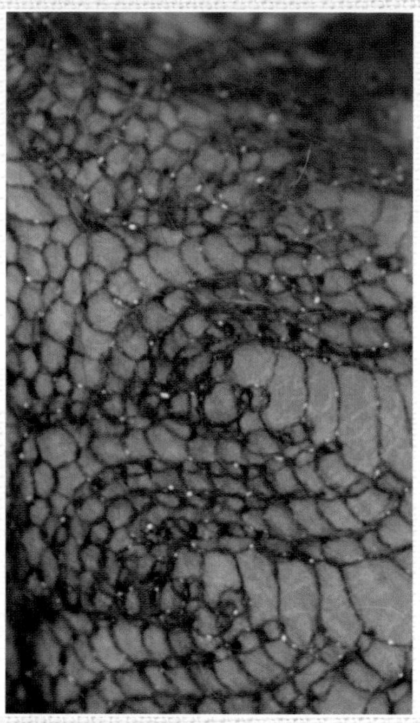

Looking at this bolero vest, it's hard to believe it's actually made from two rectangles. The edging is knit first, as a long rectangle. (If you get tired, you can stop now and have a wonderful scarf!) The resulting rectangle is seamed together at the short ends to create a circle. A back panel is picked up and worked, leaving openings for the armholes. Because the edging must be reversible (at the neck it folds back to create a collar), I again turned to the Japanese stitch patterns. This is a bit more challenging, with lace on both sides of the work. But, once you get used to the pattern, it becomes very rhythmic. The stitch motif used for the back panel comes from Estonia and is used in many Estonian lace motifs. Used alone, it creates a lovely allover fabric (another great scarf idea!).

This pattern is sized according to your cross back measurement, not the total chest measurement. This measurement is dependent on your bone structure, not your weight, so be sure to take the time to measure carefully between your shoulder bones to get the correct size. If you would like the front to be wider, just cast on 29 more stitches for the edging and add an extra repeat across (this will make the edging about 5 inches [12.7cm] wider).

SIZES

Small (Medium, Large)

FINISHED MEASUREMENTS

Cross back 13 (14, 15)"/33 (35.5, 38)cm

MATERIALS AND TOOLS

S. Charles Collezione Luna (71% super kid mohair, 20% silk, 9% lurex; 0.88oz/25g = 232yds/212.5m): 3 (3, 4) balls, color Stormy Skies #23—approx 550 (650, 750)yds/503 (594.5, 686)m of fingering weight yarn (0)

Knitting needles: 4.5mm (size 7 U.S.) or size to obtain gauge

Stitch markers

Coilless safety pins or waste yarn

Tapestry needle

GAUGE

35 sts/24 rows over chart = 7"/18cm wide x 5¼"/13.5cm tall, washed and blocked
23 sts/22 rows = 4"/10cm over Star Stitch, washed and blocked
Always take time to check your gauge.

Note

All rows are charted.

Special Abbreviations

2/2: Into the next 2 sts, work k2tog, *do not drop sts off left needle*, knit the same 2 sts together through the back loop, drop sts off left needle (2 sts made using 2 sts).

PATTERN STITCHES

star stitch worked over a repeat of 2 sts

Row 1 (RS): K1, (2/2) repeat across to last st, end k1.

Row 2 and all WS rows: Purl across.

Row 3: K2, (2/2) repeat across to last 2 sts, end k2.

Repeat rows 1–4.

INSTRUCTIONS

edging (collar and peplum)

Cast on 64 sts.

Work chart rows 1–6 64 (70, 76) times, then work row 1 once more, repeating highlighted sts twice in each row.

At the same time, place coiless safety pins at left selvedge edge after completing repeats 12 (13, 14), 19 (21, 23), 44 (48, 52), and 51 (56, 61). These markers will be referred to as markers A, B, C, and D in order of placement. Bind off loosely purlwise.

Block piece to 13½ x 84 (92, 100)"/34.5 x 213.5 (233.5, 254)cm.

Seam edging cast on edge to bind off edge.

back panel

With RS facing, beginning at marker D, pick up and knit 76 (82, 88) sts between markers D and A. Turn.

Purl 1 WS row.

work star stitch

Row 1 (RS): K1, (2/2) repeat across to last st, end k1.

Row 2 and all WS rows: Purl across.

Row 3: K2, (2/2) repeat across to last 2 sts, end k2.

Repeat rows 1–4 until piece measures 7½ (8, 8½)"/19 (20.5, 21.5)cm from pick up row. Bind off loosely knitwise.

FINISHING

Sew bind off edge of back panel to edging, between markers B and C. The sections between markers A and B and markers C and D will remain open for armholes.

Weave in all ends.

Block piece to measurements.

Starry Nights Bolero Chart

RS: knit
WS: purl

RS: yo
WS: yo

RS: purl
WS: knit

RS: k2tog
WS: p2tog

RS: ssk
WS: p2tog, tbl

RS: p2tog, tbl
WS: ssk

repeat

All rows are charted.

Starry Nights Bolero Schematic

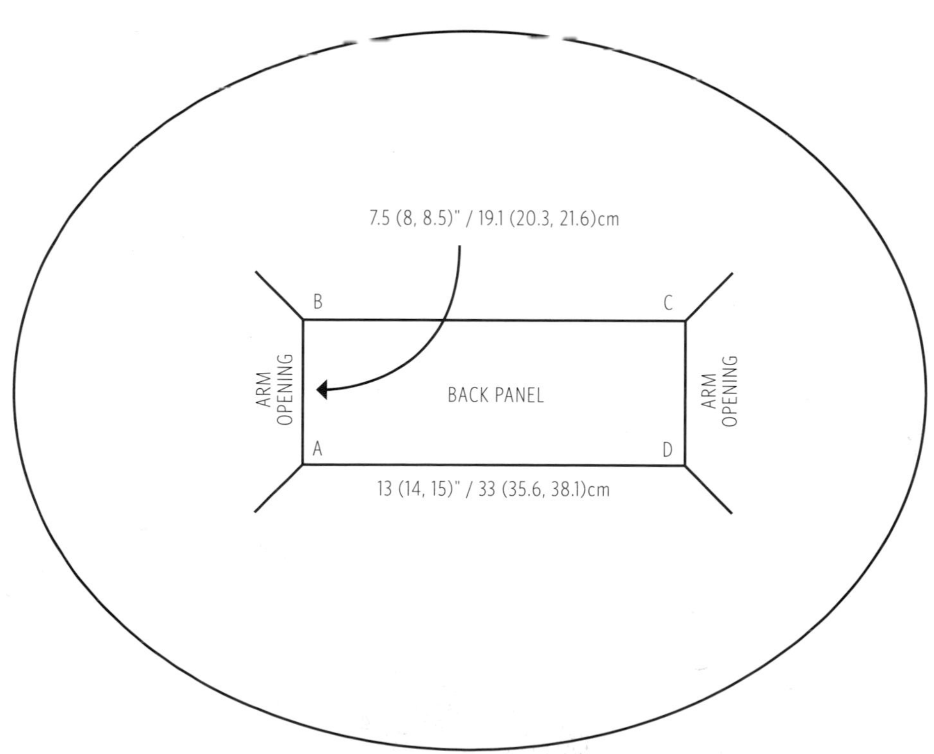

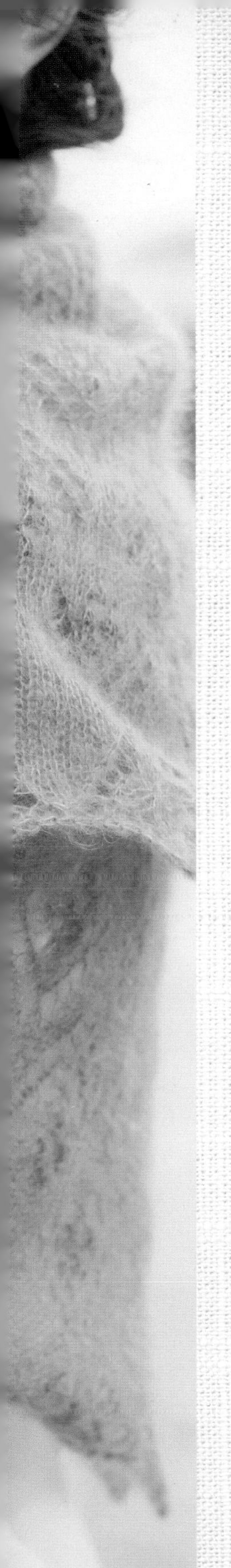

circles

CIRCLES CAN BE SHAPED in several ways. A pizza is sliced into triangles. Similarly, we can knit a circle by using six triangle shapes, knit from the center out. Elizabeth Zimmerman utilized a mathematical formula, the pi ratio, to identify a method of knitting a shawl with concentric circles. A circle can also be knit along the radius line, by working short rows (see page 19). In this chapter, we'll try our hand at each of these methods, and in the process create several stunning garments and accessories!

angel shawl

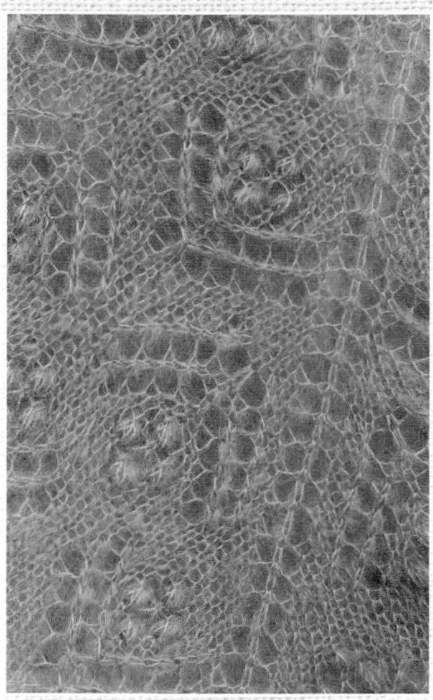

Started from the center out, this shawl makes use of the pizza wedges concept of shaping. In reality, it's a hexagon, but through the magic of blocking, we can shape it into a circle. This shape is made by knitting six triangles together. Knit from the center out, increasing 12 stitches every other round (2 stitches in each triangle) gives us the circular shape. The nupps in the stitch pattern add interest and texture and flow seamlessly into a simple edging. The size of the finished shawl can easily be adapting by altering the number of times you repeat chart 2 (page 71). To learn how to turn this shawl into a gorgeous jacket, see page 72!

FINISHED MEASUREMENTS

40"/101.5cm diameter at widest from point to point

MATERIALS AND TOOLS

Debbie Bliss Angel (76% super kid mohair, 24% silk; 0.88oz/25g = 219yd/ 200m): 4 skeins, color #19—approx 876yds/800m of sport weight yarn

Knitting needles: 3.5mm (size 4 U.S.) 1 set of 4 DPNs, 16", 32", and 47" circular needles or size to obtain gauge

Stitch markers

Tapestry needle

GAUGE

1 repeat of highlighted sts in chart 2 (14 sts/28 rows) = 3½"/9cm wide, 4½"/11.5cm tall, washed and blocked

Always take time to check your gauge.

Notes

Only odd-numbered rounds are charted; all even rounds are knit around.

7-stitch nupps are used throughout.

Shawl is worked from the center out. For directions for Belly Button cast on, see techniques (page 17). Begin with DPNs or 2 circulars using your preferred method, switching to longer needles when able.

Special Abbreviations

4 into 1 decrease: Slip 2 sts together knitwise, k2tog, pass the 2 slipped stitches over this stitch. 4 stitches decreased into 1 stitch.

INSTRUCTIONS

Using the Belly Button cast on method (page 17), cast on 6 sts. Join to work in the round, place marker for beginning of round, and knit 1 round.

Round 1: (K1, yo, PM) repeat around—12 sts.

Round 2 and all even rounds: Knit around.

Round 3: (K1, yo) repeat around—24 sts.

Round 5: (K1, yo, k3, yo) repeat around—36 sts.

Round 7: (K1, yo, k5, yo) repeat around—48 sts.

Round 9: (K1, yo, k7, yo) repeat around—60 sts.

Work chart 1 rounds 1–14, repeating chart 6 times in each round—144 sts total.

Work chart 2 rounds 1–28 twice, repeating highlighted sts as needed to marker—480 sts total.

Work chart 3 rounds 1–20, repeating highlighted sts 5 times between each set of markers.

On round 20, remove all markers except beginning of round marker—672 sts total.

Work chart 4 rounds 1–9, repeating chart 42 times around.

Round 10: Bind off knitwise, using lace bind off (see page 20).

FINISHING

Weave in all ends.

Block piece to measurements.

Angel Shawl and Poinsettia Jacket Chart 1

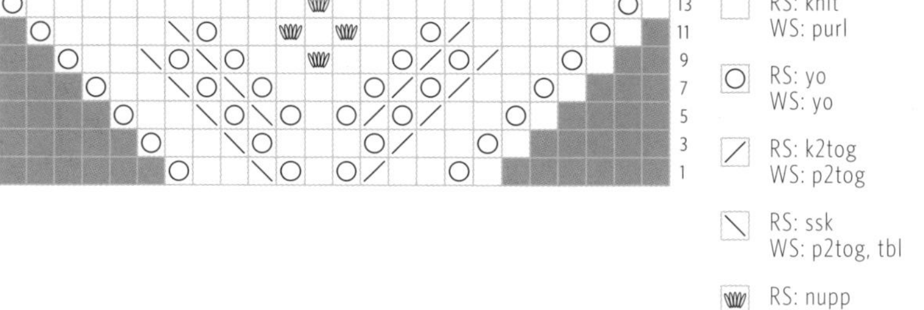

RS: knit
WS: purl

RS: yo
WS: yo

RS: k2tog
WS: p2tog

RS: ssk
WS: p2tog, tbl

RS: nupp
WS: nupp

RS: gray no stitch
WS: gray no stitch

Angel Shawl and Poinsettia Jacket Chart 2

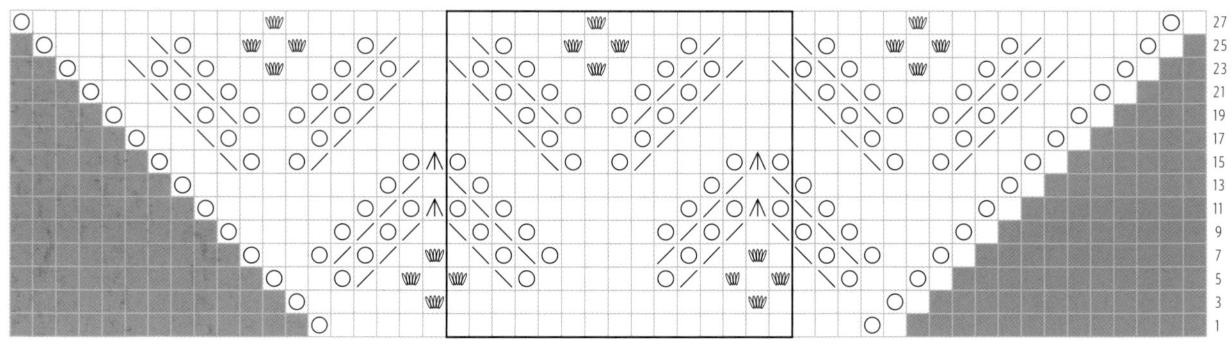

RS: knit
WS: purl

RS: yo
WS: yo

RS: k2tog
WS: p2tog

RS: ssk
WS: p2tog, tbl

RS: sl2, k1, p2sso
WS: sl2, p1, p2sso

RS: nupp
WS: nupp

RS: gray no stitch
WS: gray no stitch

repeat

Angel Shawl and Poinsettia Jacket Chart 3

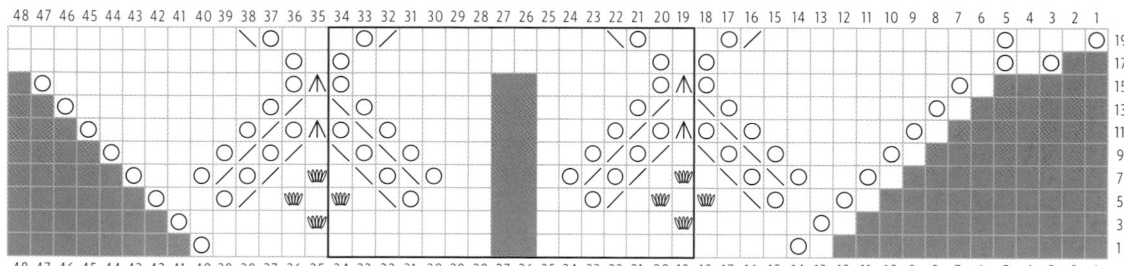

Symbol	Meaning
□	RS: knit WS: purl
○	RS: yo WS: yo
■	RS: gray no stitch WS: gray no stitch
╲	RS: ssk WS: p2tog, tbl
╱	RS: k2tog WS: p2tog
Λ	RS: sl2, k1, p2sso WS: sl2, p1, p2sso
nupp	RS: nupp WS: nupp
□	repeat

Angel Shawl and Poinsettia Jacket Chart 4

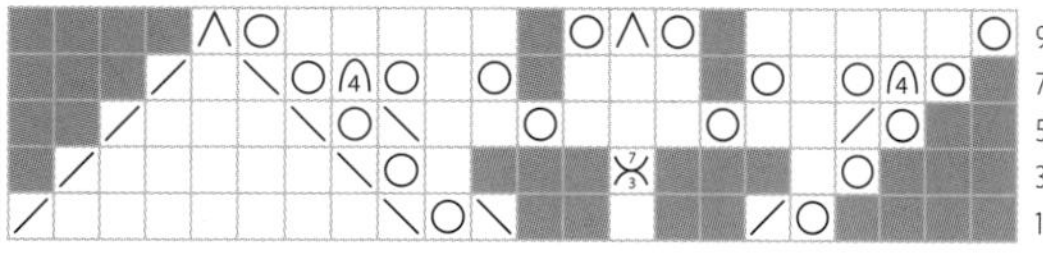

Symbol	Meaning
□	RS: knit WS: purl
○	RS: yo WS: yo
╱	RS: k2tog WS: p2tog
■	RS: gray no stitch WS: gray no stitch
╲	RS: ssk WS: p2tog, tbl
Λ	RS: sl1, k2tog, p2sso WS: sl1, wyif, p2tog, tbl, psso
3 into 7	RS: 3 into 7 gathered tbl WS: 3 into 7 gathered tbl
4	RS: 4 into 1 decrease WS: k4tog, tbl

Only odd-numbered rounds are charted; all even-numbered rounds are knit around. Shawl is worked from center out.

VARIATION

poinsettia jacket

When we add two more triangles to the Angel Shawl pattern (page 66), we get an octagon. With the added four increases every other round, this will end up with a greater than 360° circumference, or $1\frac{1}{3}$ circles! What this means practically is that the resulting fabric cannot be blocked into a two-dimensional circle and that we have added fullness and ruffles.

To turn the basic shawl into a jacket, armholes are created with waste yarn when the knitted diameter is equal to your cross back measurement, then the shawl is completed as normal. When the body is complete, the waste yarn is removed, and the sleeves are knit down to the cuff. To keep the proportions of this unique shape, multiple sizes are achieved by changing needle size and gauge. The jacket shown, a variation of the Angel Shawl, was knit using a fingering weight yarn, typically used for socks. Sizes Medium and Large could be worked in a sport weight yarn, if desired.

SIZES

Small (Medium, Large)

FINISHED MEASUREMENTS

Cross shoulder 14 (16, 18)"/35.5 (40.5, 45.5)cm
Chest 40 (46, 52)"/101.5 (117, 132)cm

MATERIALS AND TOOLS

Naturally Waikiwi (55% NZ merino, 20% nylon, 15% alpaca, 10% possum; 1.75oz/50g = 198yds/181m): 9 (11, 13) skeins, color #406—approx 1782 (2178, 2574)yds/1630 (1992, 2354)m of fingering weight yarn (1)

Knitting needles: 3.5mm (size 4 U.S.) 1 set of 5 DPNs, 16", 32", and 47" circular needles (for size Small) or size to obtain gauge

3.75mm (size 5 U.S.) (for size Medium) or size to obtain gauge

4.0mm (size 6 U.S.) (for size Large) or size to obtain gauge

Stitch markers

Waste yarn

Tapestry needle

GAUGE

1 repeat of highlighted sts in chart 2 (14 sts/28 rows) = 3½"/9cm wide, 4½"/11.5cm tall using smallest needles for size Small; 4"/10cm wide, 5¼"/13.5cm tall using middle-size needles for Medium; 4½"/11.5cm wide, 6"/15cm tall using largest needles for size Large, washed and blocked
Always take time to check your gauge.

Charts 1-4 can be found on pages 70-71. Chart 5 is on page 75.

Notes

Only odd-numbered rounds are charted; all even rounds are knit around.

7-stitch nupps are used throughout.

Jacket is worked from the center out. For directions for Belly Button cast on, see techniques (page 17). Begin with DPNs or 2 circulars using your preferred method, switching to longer needles when able.

For directions on working a w&t (wrap and turn), see page 19.

INSTRUCTIONS

Using the Belly Button cast on method, cast on 8 sts. Join to work in the round, place marker for beginning of round, and knit 1 round.

Round 1: (K1, yo, PM) repeat around—16 sts.

Round 2 and all even rounds: Knit around.

Round 3: (K1, yo) repeat around—32 sts.

Round 5: (K1, yo, k3, yo) repeat around—48 sts.

Round 7: (K1, yo, k5, yo) repeat around—64 sts.

Round 9: (K1, yo, k7, yo) repeat around—80 sts.

Work chart 1 rounds 1–14, repeating chart 8 times in each round—192 sts total.

Work chart 2 rounds 1–28, repeating highlighted sts as needed to marker—416 sts total.

armholes

Repeat chart 2 rounds 1–28, working highlighted sts 3 times between markers.

At the same time, on round 1 of chart 2, make armhole openings as follows: work in pattern to first marker, *slip marker, k1, yo (as charted), k6, knit the next 39 sts with waste yarn. Slip these 39 sts back to left needle, and knit these 39 sts again with working yarn, knit to marker, yo*. Continue in pattern as charted to 7th marker, repeat from * to * once more.

Continue working chart 2 through round 28—640 sts total.

Work chart 3 rounds 1–20, repeating highlighted sts 5 times between each set of markers.

On round 20, remove all markers except beginning of round marker—896 sts total.

Work chart 4 rounds 1–9, repeating chart 42 times around.

Round 10: Bind off knitwise, using lace bind off (page 20).

left sleeve

Remove waste yarn, placing resulting sts on 2 circular needles. You will have 39 sts on back sleeve needle, 40 sts on front sleeve needle. With RS facing, using 16" circular, join yarn at underarm and pick up and knit 1 st in gap at underarm, knit across 40 front sleeve sts, pick up and knit 1 st in gap at shoulder, knit across 39 back sleeve sts, pick up and knit 1 st in gap at underarm—82 sts. Place marker for beginning of round, join to work in the round.

shape cap

Row 1 (RS): K48, w&t.

Row 2: Slip 1, p13, w&t.

Row 3: Slip 1, k15, w&t.

Row 4: Slip 1, p17, w&t.

Continue in this manner, working 2 additional sts each row, hiding wraps as you come to them, until you have worked slip 1, p73, w&t.

Next row: Slip 1, k77, hiding wrap when you come to it. You are now at the beginning of the round, and will continue working stockinette in the round. Slip marker.

Round 1: Knit around, hiding wrap when you come to it.

Rounds 2–7: Knit around.

Round 8: K1, ssk, knit to last 2 sts, k2tog—80 sts.

Repeat rounds 2–8 nine more times—62 sts remain.

Repeat rounds 3–8 seven times—48 sts remain.

Work even on 48 sts for 4 rounds or until sleeve measures 3"/7.5cm shorter than desired length.

Work chart 5 over all sts, then work chart 4. Bind off loosely using lace bind off (page 20).

Repeat for Right Sleeve.

FINISHING

Weave in all ends.

Block piece to measurements.

Because of the unique shape of this garment, it will be necessary to block it in sections. You will not be able to get the circle to lie flat!

Poinsettia Jacket Chart 5

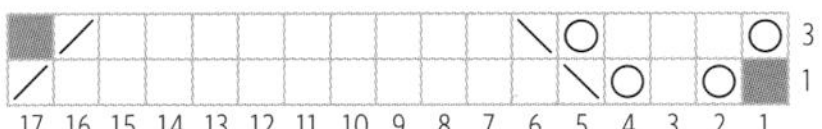

Only odd-numbered rounds are charted; all even-numbered rounds are knit around.

- RS: knit / WS: purl
- RS: gray no stitch / WS: gray no stitch
- RS: k2tog / WS: p2tog
- RS: ssk / WS: p2tog, tbl
- RS: yo / WS: yo

traveling vines cape/skirt

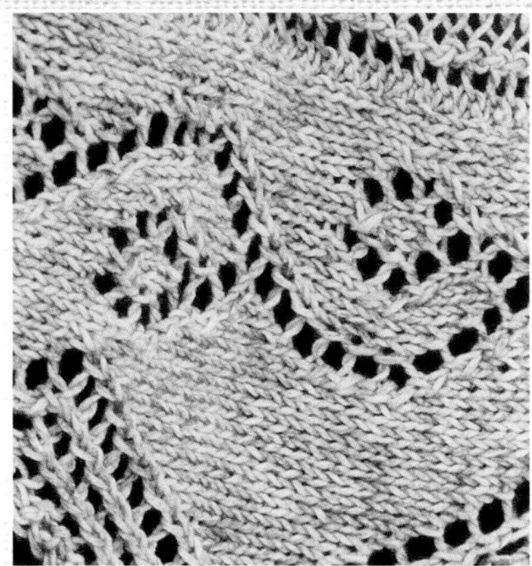

THIS PIECE IS SHAPED USING short row wedges. Knit side to side, it's an easy fit; just keep repeating the chart until it fits comfortably around your neck or waist.

A traditional Shetland edging motif forms the gentle scallops at the hem, while an Estonian floral motif meanders around the bottom of the cape. The upper section is knit in ribs of stockinette and reverse stockinette, which adds a strong vertical line to the piece. The ribs also allow us to hide the short row wraps! Rows of Shetland fagoting circle the cape, which at the top edge provides a channel for a pretty silk ribbon. Use the ribbon to gather the piece around your neck for a cape, or at the waist for a cute little skirt!

SIZES

X-Small (Small/Medium, Large, X-Large/XX-Large)

FINISHED MEASUREMENTS

Circumference at upper edge 24 (30, 36, 42)"/61 (76, 91.5, 106.5)cm

Circumference at lower edge 72 (89, 106, 123)"/183 (226, 269, 312.5)cm

Length (measured to lower scallop edge) 18"/45.5cm

MATERIALS AND TOOLS

Schachenmayr SMC Egypto Cotton Color (100% cotton; 1.75 oz/50g = 197yds/180m): 4 (5, 6, 7) skeins, color #00085—approx 788 (985, 1182, 1379)yds/720.5 (900.5, 1081, 1261)m of sock weight yarn (1)

Knitting needles: 2.75mm (size 2 U.S.) or size to obtain gauge

Tapestry needle

12 buttons, ¾"/19mm diameter

Sewing needle and thread

1½yds/1.4m of ½"/12mm-wide silk ribbon

GAUGE

24 sts/36 rows = 4"/10cm over St st, washed and blocked

Always take time to check your gauge.

Notes

Cape/skirt is knit from side to side and shaped with short rows. Because of the nature of the reverse stockinette stitch ribs, you will not need to hide your wraps on return rows.

For directions for a w&t (wrap and turn), see page 19.

All rows are charted.

INSTRUCTIONS

Cast on 84 sts.

Rows 1–4 (row 1 is RS row): Knit.

Row 5 (buttonhole row): K2, (k2tog, yo, k5) repeat across, end last repeat k3.

Rows 6–8: Knit.

Work chart rows 1–40 or written instructions below. Work rows 1–40 13 (16, 19, 22) times.

Row 1: K5, (yo, ssk) 2 times, p24, k15, (k3, yo, ssk, yo, ssk) 2 times, k5, yo, ssk, k9, (yo, ssk) 2 times, yo, k2—85 sts.

Row 2: Yo, k2tog, p21, (k3, yo, ssk, yo, ssk) 2 times, p33, w&t.

Row 3: K33, (k3, yo, ssk, yo, ssk) 2 times, k6, yo, ssk, k9, (yo, ssk) 2 times, yo, k2.

Row 4: Yo, k2tog, p22, (k3, yo, ssk) 2 times, p12, k18, w&t.

Row 5: P18, k12, (k3, yo, ssk, yo, ssk) 2 times, k7, yo, ssk, k9, (yo, ssk) 2 times, yo, k2.

Row 6: Yo, k2tog, p23, (k3, yo, ssk, yo, ssk) 2 times, p27, w&t.

Row 7: K27, (k3, yo, ssk, yo, ssk) 2 times, k5, k2tog, yo, k1, yo, ssk, k9, (yo, ssk) 2 times, yo, k2.

Row 8: Yo, k2tog, p24, (k3, yo, ssk, yo, ssk) 2 times, p9, k15, w&t.

Row 9: P15, k9, (k3, yo, ssk, yo, ssk) 2 times, k4, k2tog, yo, k3, yo, ssk, k9, (yo, ssk) 2 times, yo, k2.

Row 10: Yo, k2tog, p25, (k3, yo, ssk, yo, ssk) 2 times, p21, w&t.

Row 11: K21, (k3, yo, ssk, yo, ssk) 2 times, k4, k2tog, yo, k4, yo, ssk, k9, (yo, ssk) 2 times, yo, k2.

Row 12: Yo, k2tog, p26, (k3, yo, ssk, yo, ssk) 2 times, p6, k12, w&t.

Row 13: P12, k6, (k3, yo, ssk, yo, ssk) 2 times, k3, k2tog, yo, k1, yo, ssk, k3, yo, ssk, k9, (yo, ssk) 2 times, yo, k2.

Row 14: Yo, k2tog, p27, (k3, yo, ssk, yo, ssk) 2 times, p15, w&t.

Row 15: K15, (k3, yo, ssk, yo, ssk) 2 times, k2, k2tog, yo, k3, yo, ssk, k2, yo, ssk, k10, (yo, ssk) 2 times, yo, k2.

Row 16: Yo, k2tog, p28, (k3, yo, ssk, yo, ssk) 2 times, p3, k39, (yo, ssk) 2 times, p2—92 sts.

Row 17: K5, (yo, ssk) 2 times, p36, k3, (k3, yo, ssk, yo, ssk) 2 times, k2, k2tog, yo, k3, yo, ssk, k2, yo, ssk, k11, (yo, ssk) 2 times, yo, k2—93 sts.

Row 18: Yo, k2tog, p29, (k3, yo, ssk, yo, ssk) 2 times, p39, k3, (yo, ssk) 2 times, p2.

Row 19: K5, (yo, ssk) 2 times, k39, (k3, yo, ssk, yo, ssk) 2 times, k4, yo, sk2p, yo, k4, yo, ssk, k12, (yo, ssk) 2 times, yo, k2—94 sts.

Row 20: Yo, k2tog, p30, (k3, yo, ssk, yo, ssk) 2 times, k42, (yo, ssk) 2 times, p2.

Row 21: K5, (yo, ssk) 2 times, p39, (k3, yo, ssk, yo, ssk) 2 times, k9, k2tog, yo, k12, (k2tog, yo) 3 times, k2tog, k1—93 sts.

Row 22: Yo, k2tog, p29, (k3, yo, ssk, yo, ssk) 2 times, p15, w&t.

Row 23: K15, (k3, yo, ssk, yo, ssk) 2 times, k8, k2tog, yo, k12, (k2tog, yo) 3 times, k2tog, k1.

Row 24: Yo, k2tog, p28, (k3, yo, ssk, yo, ssk) 2 times, p3, k15, w&t.

Row 25: P15, k3, (k3, yo, ssk, yo, ssk) 2 times, k7, k2tog, yo, k12, (k2tog, yo) 3 times, k2tog, k1.

Row 26: Yo, k2tog, p27, (k3, yo, ssk, yo, ssk) 2 times, p21, w&t.

Row 27: K21, (k3, yo, ssk, yo, ssk) 2 times, k6, k2tog, yo, k1, yo, ssk, k9, (k2tog, yo) 3 times, k2tog, k1.

Row 28: Yo, k2tog, p26, (k3, yo, ssk, yo, ssk) 2 times, p6, k18, w&t.

Row 29: P18, k6, (k3, yo, ssk, yo, ssk) 2 times, k5, k2tog, yo, k3, yo, ssk, k7, (k2tog, yo) 3 times, k2tog, k1.

Row 30: Yo, k2tog, p25, (k3, yo, ssk, yo, ssk) 2 times, p27, w&t.

Row 31: K27, (k3, yo, ssk, yo, ssk) 2 times, k4, k2tog, yo, k4, yo, ssk, k6, (k2tog, yo) 3 times, k2tog, k1.

Row 32: Yo, k2tog, p24, (k3, yo, ssk, yo, ssk) 2 times, p9, k21, w&t.

Row 33: P21, k9, (k3, yo, ssk, yo, ssk) 2 times, k3, k2tog, yo, k3, k2tog, yo, k1, yo, ssk, k4, (k2tog, yo) 3 times, k2tog, k1.

Row 34: Yo, k2tog, p23, (k3, yo, ssk, yo, ssk) 2 times, p33, w&t.

Row 35: K33, (k3, yo, ssk, yo, ssk) 2 times, k3, k2tog, yo, k2, k2tog, yo, k3, yo, ssk, k2, (k2tog, yo) 3 times, k2tog, k1.

Row 36: Yo, k2tog, p22, (k3, yo, ssk, yo, ssk) 2 times, p12, k30, (yo, ssk) 2 times, p2—86 sts.

Row 37: K5, (yo, ssk) 2 times, p27, k12, (k3, yo, ssk, yo, ssk) 2 times, k3, k2tog, yo, k2, k2tog, yo, k3, yo, ssk, k1, (k2tog, yo) 3 times, k2tog, k1—85 sts.

Row 38: Yo, k2tog, p21, (k3, yo, ssk, yo, ssk) 2 times, p39, k3, (yo, ssk) 2 times, p2.

Row 39: K5, (yo, ssk) 2 times, k39, (k3, yo, ssk, yo, ssk) 2 times, k3, k2tog, yo, k4, yo, sk2p, yo, k2, (k2tog, yo) 3 times, k2tog, k1—84 sts.

Row 40: Yo, k2tog, p20, (k3, yo, ssk, yo, ssk) 2 times, p15, k27, (yo, ssk) 2 times, p2.

Rep rows 1–40 12 (15, 18, 21) more times.

Knit 8 rows.

Bind off loosely knitwise.

FINISHING

Weave in all ends.

Block piece to measurements.

Sew buttons to right front band opposite buttonholes. Weave ribbon through eyelets at upper edge.

Traveling Vines Cape/Skirt Chart

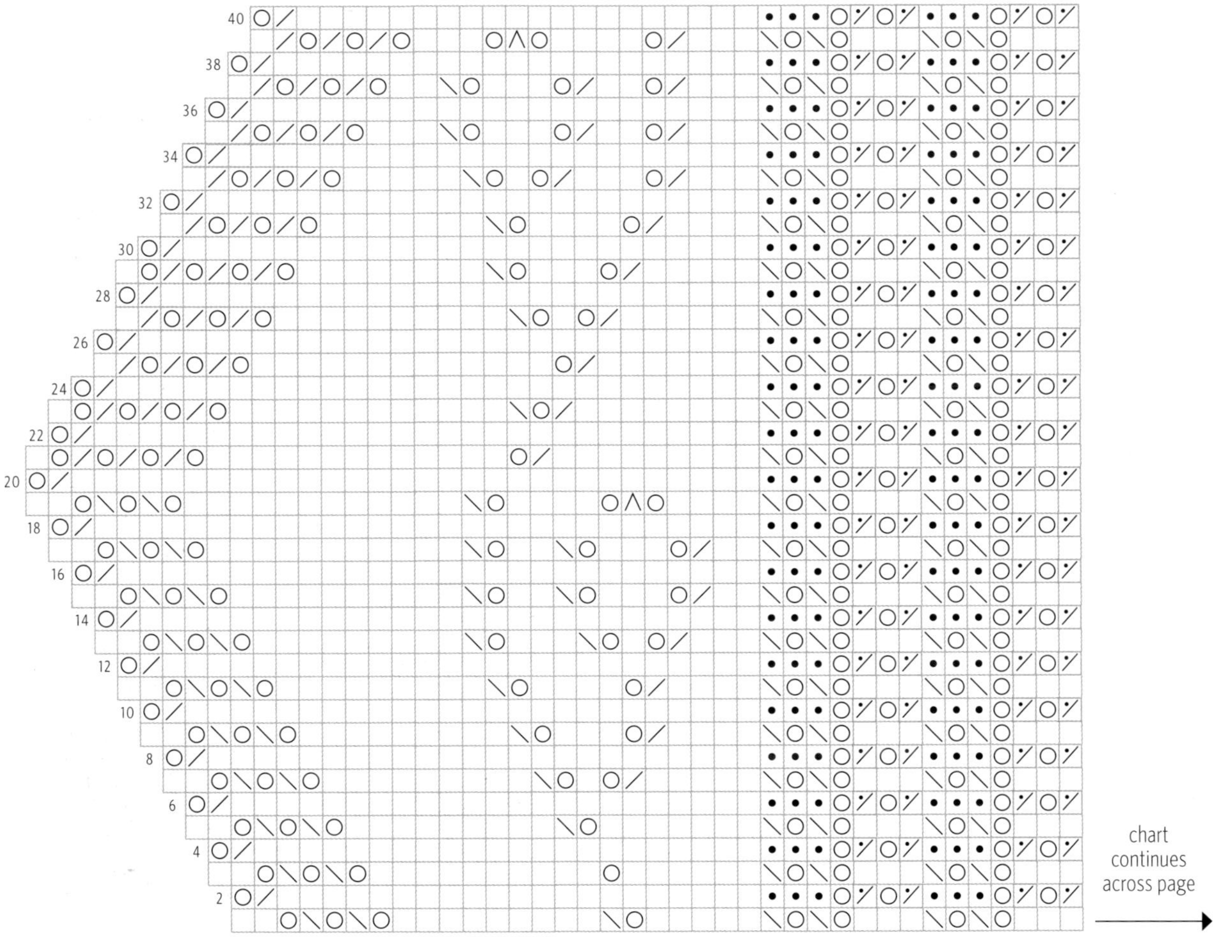

chart continues across page →

All rows are charted.

Traveling Vines Cape/Skirt Chart, continued

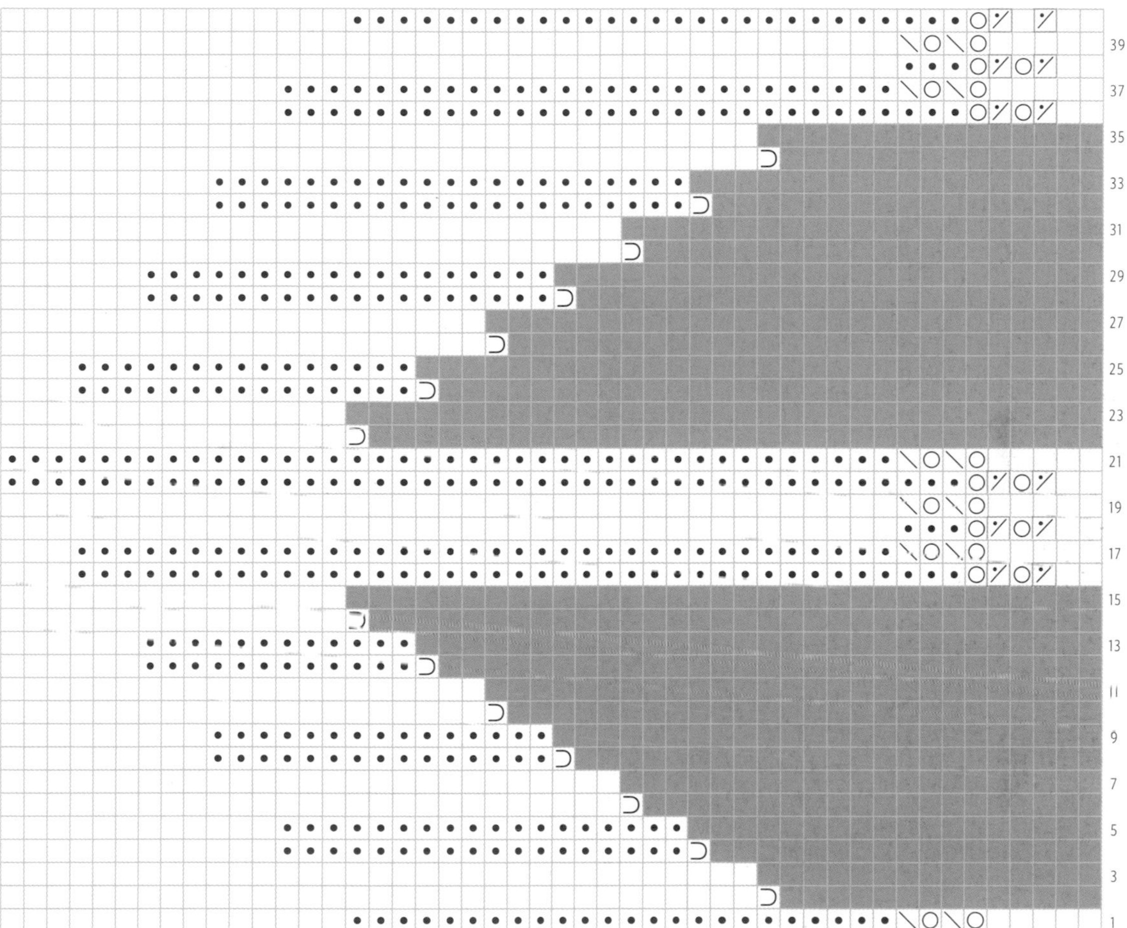

RS: knit WS: purl	RS: sl1, k2tog, psso WS: sl1, wyif, p2tog, tbl, psso
RS: yo WS: yo	RS: p2tog WS: ssk
RS: k2tog WS: p2tog	RS: purl WS: knit
RS: ssk WS: p2tog, tbl	RS: w&t WS: w&t
RS: gray no stitch WS: gray no stitch	

orange crush beret

One common method of knitting a circle is concentric circles, the most popular example being Elizabeth Zimmerman's Pi Shawl. In a nutshell, while working in garter stitch, every time you double your rounds, you will double your stitches.

The Orange Crush Beret is knit in concentric circles, however, because of the "wiggle" room we get from blocking our lace—we don't have to follow the formula with complete rigidity, because the process of blocking the finished fabric will smooth out the entire piece. In this hat, I've chosen to double the stitches on rounds 1 and 11. The next set of increases doubles the stitches, but is spread out over rounds 35 to 43 in order to blend the increases in with the lace motif. In addition, the center of the circle starts with 20 stitches, not the traditional 6 stitches. Practically, this makes the beginning of the hat much easier! It also gathers the center top of the hat into a nice little button.

FINISHED MEASUREMENTS

10"/25.5cm diameter at widest point, 6½"/16.5cm diameter at brim, unstretched

MATERIALS AND TOOLS

Lotus Yarns Mimi (100% mink; 1.75oz/50g = 328yds/300m): 1 skein, color #13—approx 328yds/300m of sport weight yarn (2)

Knitting needles: 3.25mm (size 3 U.S.) 1 set of 5 DPNs, 16" circular or size to obtain gauge

2.25mm (size 1 U.S.) 16" circular

Waste yarn

Stitch markers

Crochet hook 3.25mm (size D/3 U.S.) (for provisional cast on)

Tapestry needle

GAUGE

Over chart, using 3.25mm (size 3 U.S.) needles, rows 13–33 (20 sts/24 rows) = 4"/10cm, washed and blocked

Always take time to check your gauge.

Notes

Only odd-numbered rows are charted; all even-numbered rows are knit around.

Work the stitches as they are presented (knit the knits and yarn overs, and purl the purls).

INSTRUCTIONS

With waste yarn and 3.25mm (size D/3 U.S.) crochet hook, using provisional cast on method (page 16), cast on 20 sts.

Using DPNs, join working yarn, leaving 12"/30.5cm tail, and knit across 20 sts. Place marker and join to work in the round. Knit 1 set-up round on 20 sts.

Round 1: (K1, yo) repeat around—40 sts.

Round 2 and all even rounds to round 24: Knit around.

Rounds 3, 5, 7, and 9: (Ssk, yo) repeat around.

Round 11: Repeat round 1—80 sts.

Work chart rounds 13–72 or written directions below, repeating chart 8 times around—160 sts.

Round 13: *(Yo, ssk) 2 times, yo, sk2p, yo, k2tog, yo, k1, PM; repeat from * around.

Round 14 and all even rounds to round 22: Knit around.

Round 15: *K1, (yo, ssk) 2 times, k1, (k2tog, yo) 2 times; repeat from * around.

Round 17: (K2, yo, ssk, yo, sk2p, yo, k2tog, yo, k1) repeat around.

Round 19: (K3, yo, ssk, k1, k2tog, yo, k2) repeat around.

Round 21: (K4, yo, sk2p, yo, k3) repeat around.

Rounds 23, 25, 27, 29, and 31: (P1, ssk, k2, yo, k1, yo, k2, k2tog) repeat around.

Rounds 24, 26, 28, 30, and 32: (P1, k9) repeat around.

Round 33: (K1, yo, ssk, k5, k2tog, yo) repeat around.

Round 34 and all even rounds to round 46: Knit around.

Round 35: (K1, yo, k1, yo, ssk, k3, k2tog, yo, k1, yo) repeat around—96 sts.

Round 37: *K1, yo, k1, (yo, ssk) 2 times, k1, (k2tog, yo) 2 times, k1, yo; repeat from * around—112 sts.

Round 39: *K1, yo, k1, (yo, ssk) 2 times, yo, sk2p, yo, (k2tog, yo) 2 times, k1, yo; repeat from * around—128 sts.

Round 41: *K1, yo, k1, (yo, ssk) 3 times, k1, (k2tog, yo) 3 times, k1, yo; repeat from * around—144 sts.

Round 43: *K1, yo, k1, (yo, ssk) 3 times, yo, sk2p, yo, (k2tog, yo) 3 times, k1, yo; repeat from * around—160 sts.

Rounds 45–62: Repeat rounds 17–34.

Round 63: *(Yo, ssk) 2 times, k3, k2tog, yo, k1; repeat from * around.

Round 64: Knit around.

Rounds 65–72: Repeat rounds 15–21, removing markers as you work the last round.

Switch to 2.25mm (size 1 U.S.) needle. Knit 1 round.

Next round: (K3, k2tog) repeat around—128 sts.

Knit 3 rounds even.

Next round: (K2, p2tog) repeat around—96 sts.

Work 1"/2.5cm in k2, p1 rib. Bind off loosely using lace bind off in rib pattern as follows:

K2, slip these 2 sts back to left needle, k2togtbl, p1, slip 2 sts back to left needle, p2tog, *(k1, slip 2 sts back to left needle, k2tog tbl) 2 times, p1, slip 2 sts back to left needle, p2tog *. Repeat from * to * around. Fasten off last st.

FINISHING

Thread tapestry needle with working yarn from initial cast on. Remove provisional cast on. At the same time, pull tapestry needle with working yarn through live stitches as they are exposed. When all the waste yarn has been removed and all live stitches gathered onto working yarn, pull yarn gently to gather cast on stitches and close the hole. Weave in all ends.

Block hat over a dinner plate to shape into beret.

Orange Crush Beret Chart

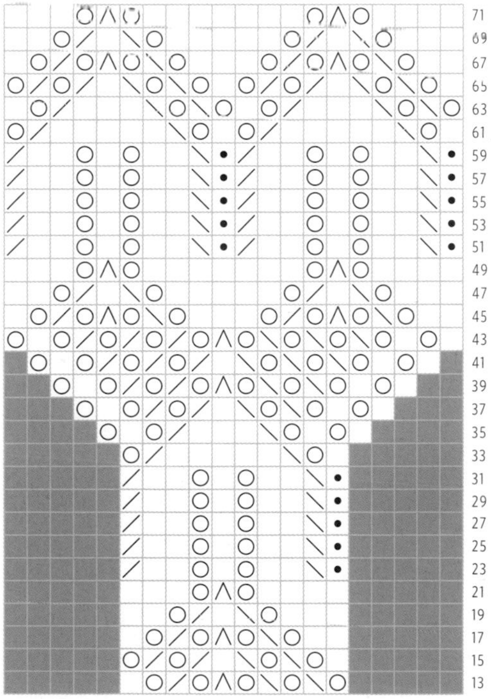

RS: knit
WS: purl

RS: yo
WS: yo

RS: gray no stitch
WS: gray no stitch

RS: k2tog
WS: p2tog

RS: ssk
WS: p2tog, tbl

RS: purl
WS: knit

RS: sl1, k2tog, psso
WS: sl1, wyif, p2tog, tbl, psso

Only odd-numbered rows are charted; all even-numbered rows are knit around. Work the stitches as they are presented (knit the knits and yarn overs, and purl the purls).

camellia dolman

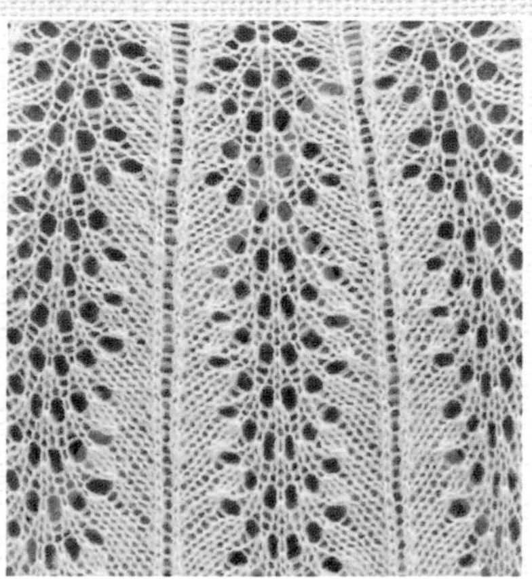

This cape is shaped with 18 rays that emanate from the neckline and increase to the hem. The rays increase at a rate of 36 stitches every six rows, which slowly shapes the circle. The secret in this garment is the finishing. After blocking, the hem is seamed together, leaving openings for the hips and arms, which gives us a great dolman sleeve shape. This cape fits nicely at the hips and stays on no matter how much you move!

This is an extremely easy knit, with a lace motif that is constant and repetitive and easy to predict. The repetition also makes it a great project for beginners to lace charts.

FINISHED MEASUREMENTS

Circumference at hem 144"/366cm
Length from shoulder 28"/71cm

MATERIALS AND TOOLS

Filatura Di Crosa Superior (70% cashmere, 25% silk, 5% extrafine merino wool; 0.88oz/25g = 328yds/300m): (A), 5 balls, color #01—approx 3000yds/2743m of lace yarn weight (0)

Filatura Di Crosa Nirvana (100% extrafine merino superwash mercerized; 0.88oz/25g = 372yds/340m): (B), 4 balls, color #01—approx 3000yds/2743m of lace weight yarn (0)

Knitting needles: 3.25mm (size 3 U.S.) 24" circular

3.75mm (size 5 U.S.) 32" or 40" circular or size to obtain gauge

Stitch markers

Coiless safety pins

7 buttons, ¾"/19mm diameter

Sewing needle and thread

Tapestry needle

GAUGE

18 sts/26 rows = 4"/10cm using larger needles and 1 strand each of A and B held together, washed and blocked
Always take time to check your gauge.

Notes

Garment is worked with 1 strand each of A and B held together throughout.

Only odd-numbered rows are charted; all even rows are purl across.

This is a one-size-fits-all garment. Instructions in the finishing allow you to fit the finished garment to a hip measurement of 32 (40, 48, 56, 64)"/81.5 (101.5, 122, 142, 162.5)cm.

Note special instructions regarding rows 159, 167, 175, and 183 in chart.

INSTRUCTIONS

Cast on 78 sts using 3.25mm (size 3 U.S.) needle.

Row 1 (WS): P3, (k2, p2) repeat across, end p3.

Row 2: K3, (k2, p2) repeat across, end k3.

Repeat rows 1 and 2 twice more.

Next row: P3, PM, (p4, PM) repeat across, end p3.

Switch to 3.75mm (size 5 U.S.) needle.

Work chart, or follow written instructions below, working first and last 3 stitches of each row in St st, repeating chart 18 times across each row.

Bind off loosely on row 188.

chart

Row 1: K3, (k2, yo, k2) repeat across, end k3—96 sts.

Row 2 and all WS rows: Purl across.

Rows 3, 7, and 11: Knit across.

Rows 5 and 9: K3, (ssk, yo, k1, yo, k2tog) repeat across, end k3.

Row 13: K3, (ssk, yo, into the next st work [k1, yo, k1], yo, k2tog) repeat across, end k3—132 sts.

Row 15: Knit across.

Rows 17 and 21: K3, *ssk, yo, (k1, yo) 3 times, k2tog; repeat from * across, end k3—168 sts.

Rows 19 and 23: K3, (ssk, k5, k2tog), repeat across, end k3—132 sts.

Row 25: K3, (ssk, yo, k1, yo, into next st work [k1, yo, k1], yo, k1, yo, k2tog) repeat across, end k3—204 sts.

Rows 27 and 31: K3, (ssk, k7, k2tog) repeat across, end k3—168 sts.

Row 29: K3, *ssk, (k1, yo) 4 times, k1, k2tog; repeat from * across, end k3.

Row 33: K3, *ssk, yo, (k1, yo) 5 times, k2tog; repeat from * across, end k3—240 sts.

Rows 35 and 39: K3, (ssk, k9, k2tog) repeat across, end k3—204 sts.

Row 37: K3, *ssk, k2, (yo, k1) 4 times, k1, k2tog; repeat from * across, end k3—240 sts.

Row 41: K3, *ssk, (k1, yo) 6 times, k1, k2tog; repeat from * across, end k3—276 sts.

Rows 43 and 47: K3, (ssk, k11, k2tog) repeat across, end k3—240 sts.

Row 45: K3, *ssk, k3, (yo, k1) 4 times, k2, k2tog; repeat from * across, end k3—276 sts.

Row 49: K3, *ssk, k2, (yo, k1) 6 times, k1, k2tog; repeat from * across, end k3—312 sts.

Rows 51, 55, and 59: K3, (ssk, k13, k2tog) repeat across, end k3—276 sts.

Rows 53 and 57: K3, *ssk, k1, k2tog, (yo, k1) 5 times, yo, ssk, k1, k2tog; repeat from * across, end k3—312 sts.

Row 61: K3, *ssk, k3, (yo, k1) 6 times, k2, k2tog; repeat from * across, end k3—348 sts.

Rows 63, 67, and 71: K3, (ssk, k15, k2tog) repeat across, end k3—312 sts.

Rows 65 and 69: K3, *ssk, k2, k2tog, (yo, k1) 5 times, yo, ssk, k2, k2tog; repeat from * across, end k3—348 sts.

Row 73: K3, *ssk, k4, (yo, k1) 6 times, k3, k2tog; repeat from * across, end k3—384 sts.

Rows 75, 79, and 83: K3, (ssk, k17, k2tog) repeat across, end k3—348 sts.

Rows 77 and 81: K3, *ssk, k3, k2tog, (yo, k1) 5 times, yo, ssk, k3, k2tog; repeat from * across, end k3—384 sts.

Row 85: K3, *ssk, k5 (yo, k1) 6 times, k4, k2tog; repeat from * across, end k3—420 sts.

Rows 87, 91, and 95: K3, (ssk, k19, k2tog), repeat across, end k3—384 sts.

Rows 89 and 93: K3, *ssk, k4, k2tog, (yo, k1) 5 times, yo, ssk, k4, k2tog; repeat from * across, end k3—420 sts.

Row 97: K3, *ssk, k6, (yo, k1) 6 times, k5, k2tog; repeat from * across, end k3—456 sts.

Rows 99, 103, and 107: K3, (ssk, k21, k2tog) repeat across, end k3—420 sts.

Rows 101 and 105: K3, *ssk, k5, k2tog, (yo, k1) 5 times, yo, ssk, k5, k2tog; repeat from * across, end k3—456 sts.

Row 109: K3, *ssk, k7, (yo, k1) 6 times, k6, k2tog; repeat from * across, end k3—492 sts.

Rows 111, 115, and 119: K3, (ssk, k23, k2tog) repeat across, end k3—456 sts.

Rows 113 and 117: K3, *ssk, k6, k2tog, (yo, k1) 5 times, yo, ssk, k6, k2tog; repeat from * across, end k3—492 sts.

Row 121: K3, *ssk, k8, (yo, k1) 6 times, k7, k2tog; repeat from * across, end k3—528 sts.

Rows 123, 127, and 131: K3, (ssk, k25, k2tog) repeat across, end k3—492 sts.

Rows 125 and 129: K3, *ssk, k7, k2tog, (yo, k1) 5 times, yo, ssk, k7, k2tog; repeat from * across, end k3—528 sts.

Row 133: K3, *ssk, k9, (yo, k1) 6 times, k8, k2tog; repeat from * across, end k3—564 sts.

Rows 135, 139, and 143: K3, (ssk, k27, k2tog) repeat across, end k3—528 sts.

Rows 137 and 141: K3, *ssk, k8, k2tog, (yo, k1) 5 times, yo, ssk, k8, k2tog; repeat from * across, end k3—564 sts.

Row 145: K3, *ssk, k10, (yo, k1) 6 times, k9, k2tog; repeat from * across, end k3—600 sts.

Rows 147 and 151: K3, (ssk, k29, k2tog) repeat across, end k3—564 sts.

Row 149: K3, *ssk, k9, k2tog, (yo, k1) 5 times, yo, ssk, k9, k2tog; repeat from * across, end k3—600 sts.

Row 153: K3, *yo, ssk, k11, (yo, k1) 6 times, k10, k2tog; repeat from * across, end yo, k3—655 sts.

Row 155: K3, (k1, yo, ssk, k31, k2tog, yo) repeat across, end yo, k4.

Row 157: K3, *k2, yo, ssk, k10, k3tog, (yo, k1) 3 times, yo, sk2p, k10, k2tog, yo, k1; repeat from * across, end k4.

Row 159: K3, k2tog, (yo, k1, yo, ssk, k27, k2tog, yo, k1, yo, sk2p) repeat across, end last repeat ssk, k3.

Row 161: K3, *k4, yo, ssk, k8, k3tog, (yo, k1) 3 times, yo, sk2p, k8, k2tog, yo, k3; repeat from * across, end k4.

Row 163: K3, (k1, yo, sk2p, yo, k1, yo, ssk, k23, k2tog, yo, k1, yo, sk2p, yo) repeat across, end k4.

Row 165: K3, *k6, yo, ssk, k6, k3tog, (yo, k1) 3 times, yo, sk2p, k6, k2tog, yo, k5; repeat from * across, end k4.

Row 167: K3, k2tog, (yo, k1, yo, sk2p, yo, k1, yo, ssk, k19, k2tog, yo, k1, yo, sk2p, yo, k1, yo, sk2p) repeat across, end last repeat ssk, k3.

Row 169: K3, *k8, yo, ssk, k4, k3tog, (yo, k1) 3 times, yo, sk2p, k4, k2tog, yo, k7; repeat from * across, end k4.

Row 171: K3, *k1, (yo, sk2p, yo, k1) 2 times, yo, ssk, k15, k2tog, yo, (k1, yo, sk2p, yo) 2 times; repeat from * across, end k4.

Row 173: K3, *k10, yo, ssk, k2, k3tog, (yo, k1) 3 times, yo, sk2p, k2, k2tog, yo, k9; repeat from * across, end k4.

Row 175: K3, k2tog, *yo, k1, (yo, sk2p, yo, k1) 2 times, yo, ssk, k11, k2tog, yo, k1, (yo, sk2p, yo, k1) 2 times, yo, sk2p; repeat from * across, end last repeat ssk, k3.

Row 177: K3, (k12, yo, ssk, k9, k2tog, yo, k11) repeat across, end k4.

Row 179: K3, *k1, (yo, sk2p, yo, k1) 3 times, yo, ssk, k7, k2tog, yo, (k1, yo, sk2p, yo) 3 times; repeat from * across, end k4.

Row 181: K3, (k14, yo, ssk, k5, k2tog, yo, k13) repeat across, end k4.

Row 183: K3, k2tog, *yo, k1, (yo, sk2p yo, k1) 3 times, yo, ssk, k3, k2tog, yo, k1, (yo, sk2p, yo, k1) 3 times, yo, sk2p; repeat from * across, end last repeat ssk, k3.

Row 185: K3, (k16, yo, ssk, k1, k2tog, yo, k15) repeat across, end k4.

Row 187: K3, (k1, yo, sk2p, yo) repeat across, end k4.

left front band

With RS facing and smaller 24" needle, pick up and knit 130 sts in left front selvedge edge.

Knit 1 WS row.

Next row (buttonhole row): K4, yo, k2tog, (k18, yo, k2tog) repeat to last 4 sts, k4.

Knit 2 rows.

Bind off loosely knitwise.

right front band

With RS facing and smaller 24" needle, pick up and knit 130 sts in right front selvedge edge.

Knit 4 rows.

Bind off loosely.

Block piece to measurements.

Starting at left center front, place coiless safety pins along lower edge at the following points:

after 8 (10, 12, 14, 16)"/20.5 (25.5, 30.5, 35.5, 40.5)cm, marker A (left front)

after 32 (32, 32, 32, 32)"/81 (81, 81, 81, 81)cm, marker B (left front seam)

after 40 (40, 40, 40, 40)"/101.5 (101.5, 101.5, 101.5, 101.5)cm, marker C (arm opening)

after 64 (62, 60, 58, 56)"/162.5 (157.5, 152.5, 147.5, 142)cm, marker D (left back seam)

after 80 (82, 84, 86, 88)"/203 (208, 213.5, 218.5, 223.5)cm, marker E (back)

after 104 (104, 104, 104, 104)"/264 (264, 264, 264, 264)cm, marker F (right back seam)

after 112 (112, 112, 112, 112)"/284.5 (284.5, 284.5, 284.5, 284.5)cm, marker G (right arm opening)

after 136 (134, 132, 130, 128)"/345.5 (340.5, 335, 330, 325)cm, marker H (right back seam)

8 (10, 12, 14, 16)"/20.5 (25.5, 30.5, 35.5, 40.5)cm remain to right center front (right front)

Seam bind off sts between markers A and B to bind off sts between markers C and D. Seam bind off sts between markers E and F to bind off sts between markers G and H. Remove all markers.

FINISHING

Weave in all ends.

Sew buttons to right front band opposite buttonholes.

Camellia Dolman Schematic

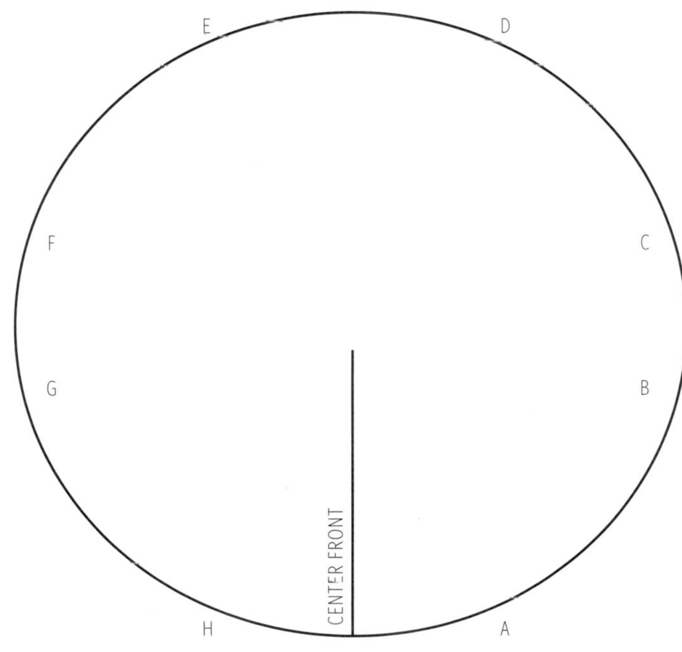

Center to A: 8 (10, 12, 14, 16)" / 20.3 (25.4, 30.5, 35.6, 40.6)cm
A to B: 24 (22, 20, 18, 16)" / 61 (55.9, 50.8, 45.7, 40.6)cm
B to C: 8" / 20.3 cm
C to D: 24 (22, 20, 18, 16)" / 61 (55.9, 50.8, 45.7, 40.6)cm
D to E: 16 (20, 24, 28, 32)" / 40.6 (50.8, 61, 71.1, 81.3)cm
E to F: 24 (22, 20, 18, 16)" / 61 (55.9, 50.8, 45.7, 40.6)cm
F to G: 8" / 20.3 cm
G to H: 24 (22, 20, 18, 16)" / 61 (55.9, 50.8, 45.7, 40.6)cm
H to center: 8 (10, 12, 14, 16)" / 20.3 (25.4, 30.5, 35.6, 40.6)cm

Camellia Dolman Chart

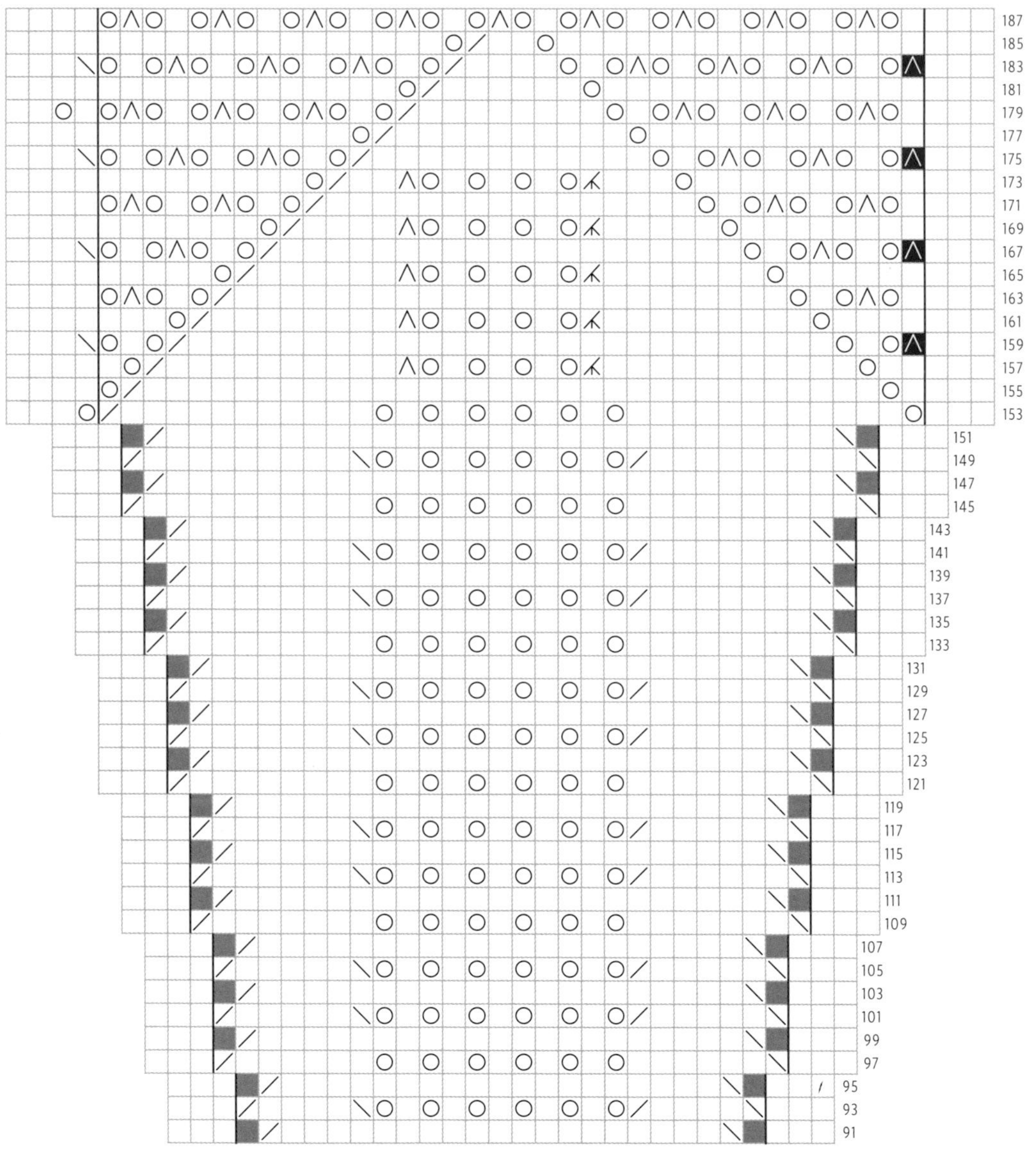

chart continues
on next page

Camellia Dolman Chart, continued

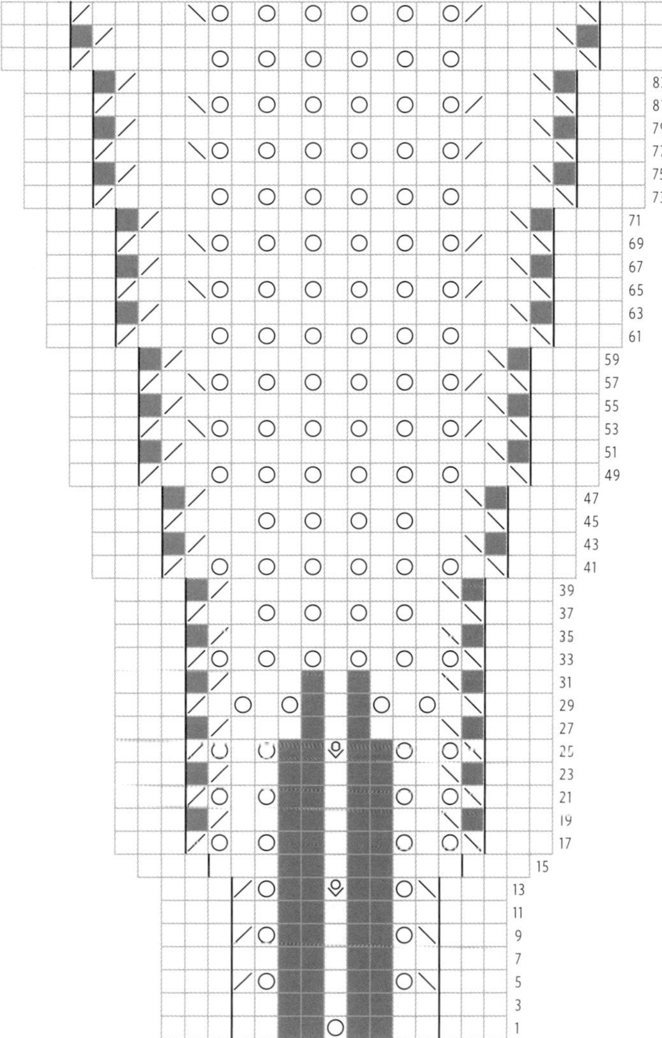

- [black square with ∧] on 1st repeat of these rows, work this st as k2tog
- [white square] RS: knit / WS: purl
- [O] RS: yo / WS: yo
- [∧] RS: sl1, k2tog, psso / WS: sl1, wyif, p2tog, tbl, psso
- [gray square] RS: gray no stitch / WS: gray no stitch
- [•] RS: purl / WS: knit
- [/] RS: k2tog / WS: p2tog
- [\] RS: ssk / WS: p2tog, tbl
- [(k1, yo, k1) symbol] RS: (k1, yo, k1) in 1 stitch / WS: p1, yo, p1, in 1 stitch
- [k3tog symbol] RS: k3tog / WS: p3tog
- [outlined box] repeat

Only odd-numbered rows are charted; all even-numbered rows are purl across.

squares

LIKE THE RECTANGLE, THE SQUARE is a simple shape, and with no increases or decreases necessary, it can be made with any stitch pattern! In this chapter, we'll take that humble square and use it to create a variety of lovely garments. Although yarn and gauge are recommended, this is a great opportunity to experiment.

dahlia shawl

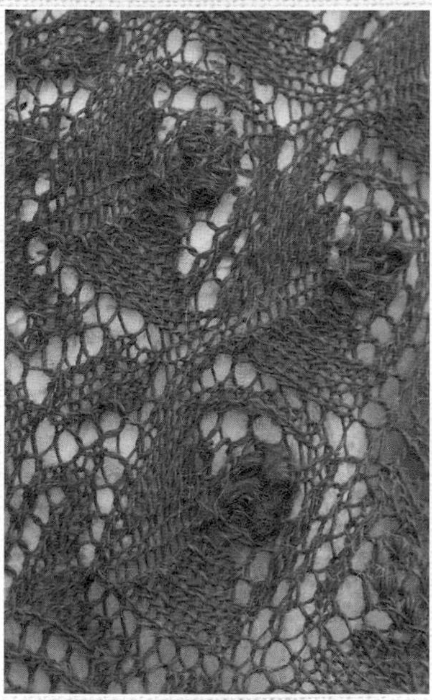

Nothing is more elegant than a sumptuous shawl draped around your shoulders! Knit in baby alpaca lace weight yarn, this shawl will add elegance and warmth to every outfit. The shawl is knit from the center out and grows from there. Look closely, and you'll notice that it is actually four triangles! You can take your favorite top-down triangle shawl, which is constructed with two triangles, and turn it into a square shawl.

FINISHED MEASUREMENTS

47"/119.5cm square

MATERIALS AND TOOLS

Zitron Fil Royal (100% baby alpaca; 3.5oz/100g = 660yds/600m).
3 skeins, color #3505—approx 1500yds/1372m of lace weight yarn (0)

Knitting needles: 3.25mm (size 3 U.S.) 1 set of 4 DPNs, 16", 32", and 47" circular needles or size to obtain gauge

Waste yarn

Stitch markers

Tapestry needle

GAUGE

1 repeat of highlighted stitches in chart 2 (16 sts/16 rows) = 3¼ x 3¼"/8.5 x 8.5cm, washed and blocked

Always take time to check your gauge.

Notes

Only odd-numbered rounds are charted; all even-numbered rounds are knit around.

For directions for Belly Button cast on, see techniques (page 17). Begin with DPNs or 2 circulars using your preferred method, switching to longer needles when able.

INSTRUCTIONS

Using Belly Button cast on method on page 17, cast on 8 sts.

Join to work in the round. Place marker for beginning of round. In set-up round, use markers of different color from beginning of round marker.

Set-up round: (K2, PM) repeat around using beginning of round marker for last marker.

Work chart 1 rounds 1–15 once, repeating chart 4 times in each round—72 sts.

Work chart 2 rounds 17–31 ten times, repeating chart 4 times in each round, and working highlighted sts as needed between markers—712 sts.

Work chart 3 rounds 1–33, working highlighted sts as needed between markers—848 sts. Bind off loosely using lace bind off on round 34.

FINISHING

Remove waste yarn from cast on, pull tail through live stitches, and fasten off. Weave in all ends.

Block piece to measurements.

Dahlia Shawl Chart 1

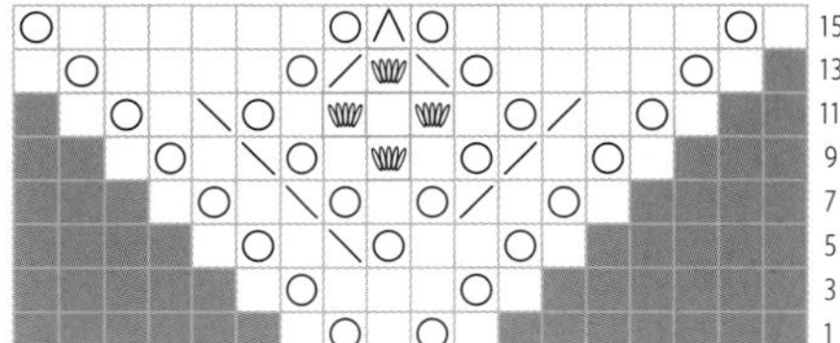

- RS: knit
  WS: purl
- RS: yo
  WS: yo
- RS: gray no stitch
  WS: gray no stitch
- RS: k2tog
  WS: p2tog
- RS: ssk
  WS: p2tog, tbl
- RS: sl1, k2tog, psso
  WS: sl1, wyif, p2tog, psso
- RS: nupp
  WS: nupp

Dahlia Shawl Chart 2

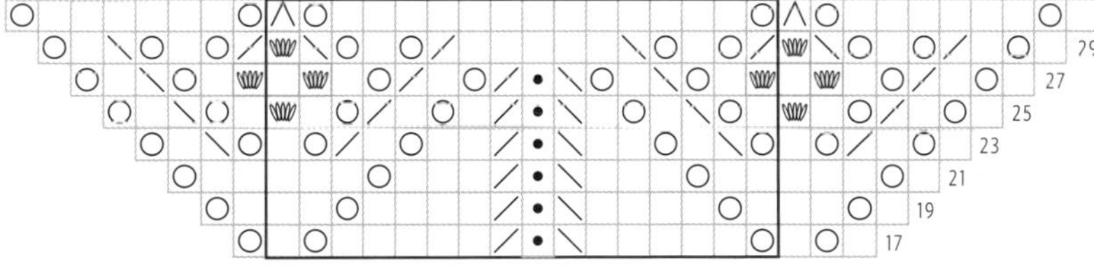

- RS: knit
  WS: purl
- RS: yo
  WS: yo
- RS: k2tog
  WS: p2tog
- RS: ssk
  WS: p2tog, tbl
- RS: purl
  WS: knit
- RS: nupp
  WS: nupp
- RS: sl1, k2tog, psso
  WS: sl1, wyif, p2tog, tbl, psso
- repeat

Only odd-numbered rounds are charted;
all even-numbered rounds are knit around.

Dahlia Shawl Chart 3

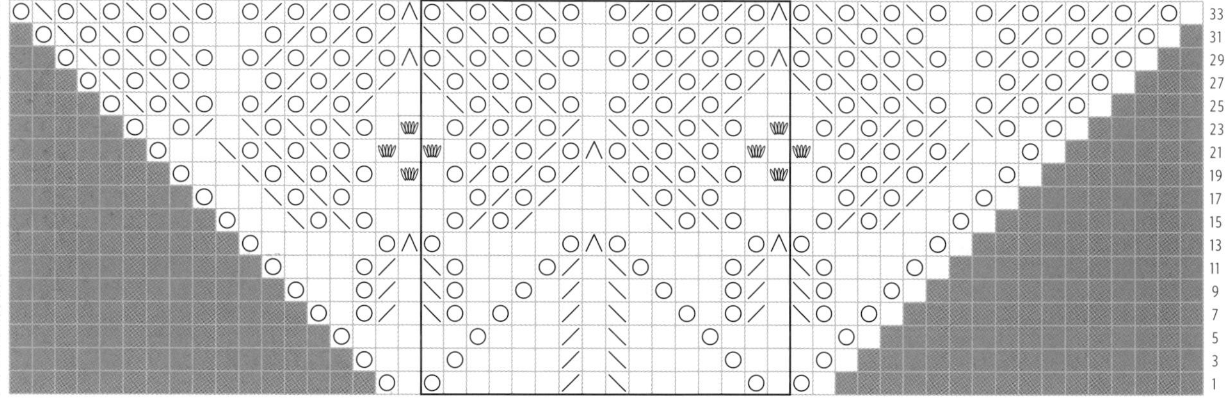

RS: knit
WS: purl

RS: yo
WS: yo

RS: k2tog
WS: p2tog

RS: ssk
WS: p2tog, tbl

RS: nupp
WS: nupp

RS: sl1, k2tog, psso
WS: sl1, wyif, p2tog, tbl, psso

repeat

RS: gray no stitch
WS: gray no stitch

aster shirt

Take two squares and seam them together at the shoulder, leaving an opening for your head. Seam the sides, and you have a lovely shirt! The unique flat fell seam, made by sewing the pieces together with the wrong sides facing each other, allows the shirt to be fitted through the torso, but loose and drapey at the upper body. This is going to be the shirt you throw on for everyday wear, then wear out for a night on the town! The yarn is a linen/cotton blend, which will give it great drape and flow. The chainette construction of the yarn helps it hold its shape and eliminates sagging. The twisted stitches and mock cables of this stitch pattern also help maintain the shape of the finished piece.

SIZES

Small (Medium/Large, X-Large/XX-Large)

FINISHED MEASUREMENTS

Bust 34 (44, 53)"/86.5 (112, 134.5)cm
Length 26"/66cm
Each panel (front and back) 26 (31, 35½) x 26"/66 (78.5, 90) x 66cm

MATERIALS AND TOOLS

Fiesta Yarns Linnette (70% linen, 30% cotton; 3.5oz/100g = 380yds/347.5m): 3 (4, 5) skeins, color Pansies—approx 1100 (TK) yds/1006 (TK)m of sock weight yarn (1)

Knitting needles: 3.5mm (size 4 U.S.) 24" circular or size to obtain gauge

Tapestry needle

Sewing needle and thread

GAUGE

28 sts/26 rows = 4"/10cm in pattern, washed and blocked
Always take time to check your gauge.

Notes

Only odd-numbered rows are charted; all even-numbered rows are purl across.

Special Abbreviations

Hook 3 stitches: Slip 1, into the next 2 stitches, work k1, yo, k1. Pass the slipped stitch over these 3 stitches.

INSTRUCTIONS

back

Cast on 181 (213, 245) sts.

Set-up row: P3, (p7, k1, p7, k1, p15, k1) repeat across, end p7, k1, p10.

Work chart rows 1–56 three times, or until panel is desired length.

Bind off all stitches. Block piece to measurements.

front

Cast on 181 (213, 245) sts.

Set-up row: P3, (p15, k1, p7, k1, p7, k1) repeat across, end p18.

Work chart rows 29–56 once, rows 1–56 twice, then rows 1–28 once.

Bind off all stitches. Block piece to measurements.

FINISHING

Sew shoulder seams, leaving 11"/28cm open at center for neck. Beginning at lower edge, sew front and back together about 4½"/11.5cm (2 pattern repeats) in from each side edge for about 11"/28cm, leaving top 15"/38cm open on each side for armholes.

Weave in all ends.

Aster Shirt Schematic

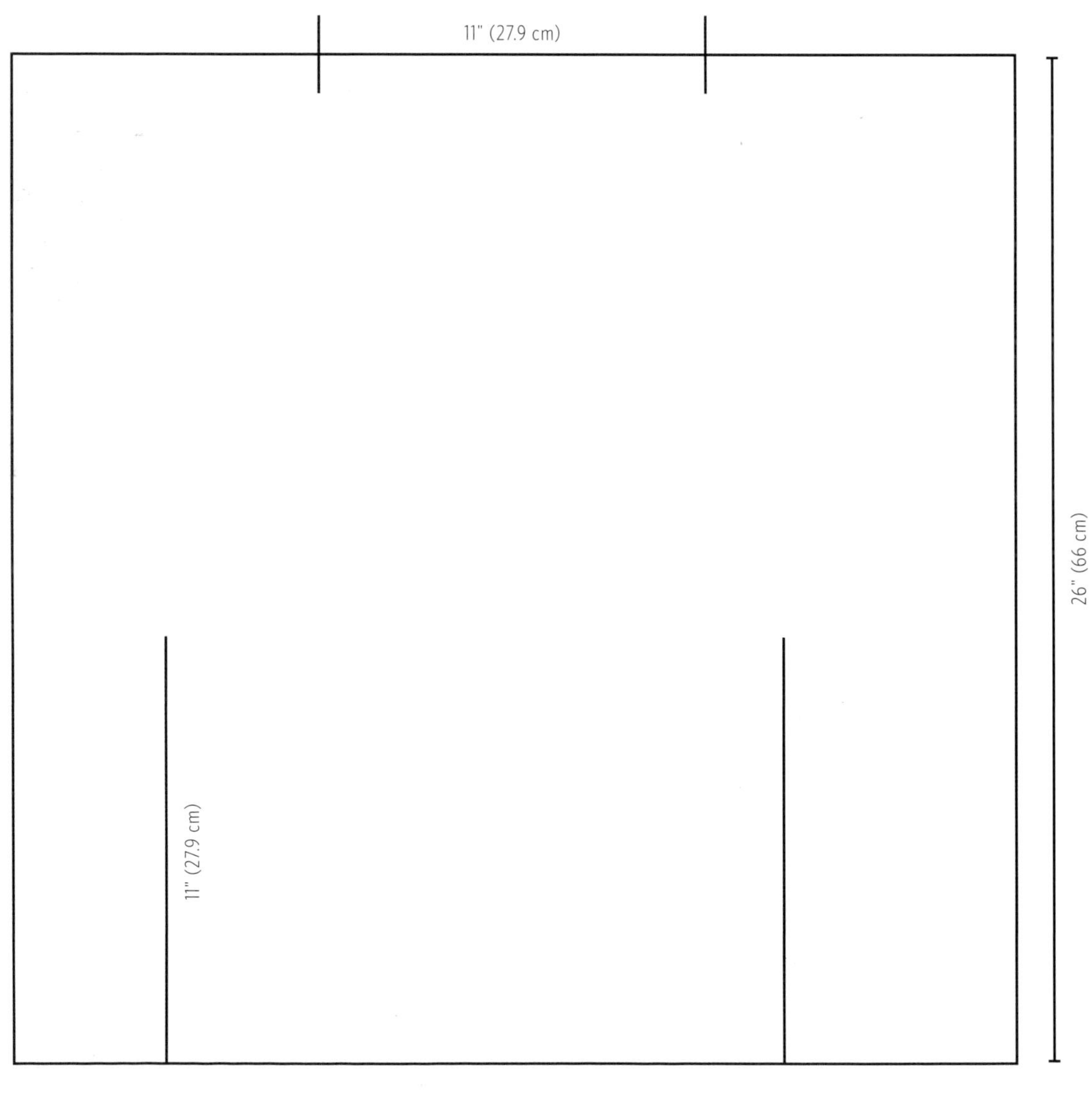

Aster Shirt Chart

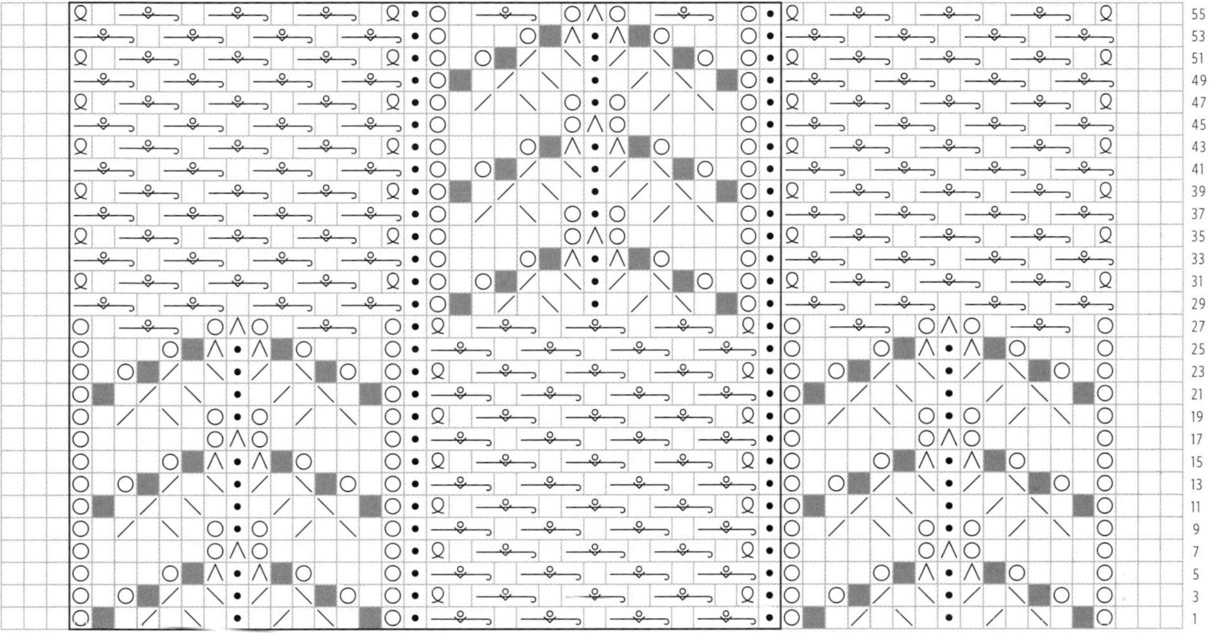

Only odd-numbered rows are charted; all even-numbered rows are purl across.

- RS: knit / WS: purl
- RS: yo / WS: yo
- RS: gray no stitch / WS: gray no stitch
- RS: ssk / WS: p2tog, tbl
- RS: k2tog / WS: p2tog
- RS: purl / WS: knit
- RS: sl1, k2tog, psso / WS: sl1, wyif, p2tog, tbl, psso
- RS: hook 3 stitches / WS: hook 3 stitches (see Special Abbreviations, page 104)
- RS: k tbl / WS: p tbl
- repeat

birch jacket

It's hard to believe this little jacket is actually based on two squares! It starts with the sleeves, which are knit from the cuff up to the sleeve cap. Short rows shape the cap of the sleeve. Then you'll join the sleeves and work half of the body out, shaping as you would a square shawl. Repeat for the other sleeve and half of the body. When both sides are completed, seam the center back, and then you can continue working around on what is now a rectangle. The linen-blend yarn is lovely to work with, providing body and structure for the jacket, but with the great drape that linen brings. A simple lace stitch makes this a pleasure to work.

SIZES

Small (Medium, Large, X-Large)

FINISHED MEASUREMENTS

Bust 36 (40, 44, 48)"/91.5 (101.5, 112, 122)cm

MATERIALS AND TOOLS

Schoppel Wolle Leinen Los (70% virgin wool, 30% linen; 3.5oz/100g = 328yds/300m): 3 (4, 4, 4) balls, color #8495—approx 900 (1000, 1100, 1200)yds/823 (914.5, 1006, 1097.5)m of light worsted weight yarn (3)

Knitting needles: 3.5mm (size 4 U.S.) 16", 32", and 60" circulars or size to obtain gauge

Stitch markers

Waste yarn

GAUGE

21 sts/30 rows = 4"/10cm, over fagot stitch pattern, washed and blocked

Always take time to check your gauge.

Notes

Only odd-numbered rows/rounds are charted. All even rows are purl across. All even rounds are knit around.

Jacket is made in two halves: right sleeve and body, and left sleeve and body. Each half is worked beginning at the wrist edge of sleeve and working toward the center back. Edging is worked around the entire outer edge of the two halves combined.

PATTERN STITCHES

fagot stitch

Worked over a repeat of 6 sts +1.

Row 1: (K1, yo, k1, sk2p, k1, yo) repeat across, end k1.

Row 2: Purl across.

right sleeve and body

Work back and forth in rows on 16" circular needle.

Cast on 41 (41, 53, 53) sts.

Work chart 1 rows 1–36 three times, then work rows 1–28 once more, repeating highlighted sts 6 (6, 8, 8) times across row—85 (85, 97, 97) sts.

shape cap

Row 1: K3, k2tog, k1, (yo, k1, yo, k1, sk2p, k1) 12 (12, 14, 14) times, yo, k1, turn (6 sts rem unworked).

Row 2: P73 (73, 85, 85), turn (6 sts rem unworked).

Row 3: K1, yo, k1, sk2p, k1, (yo, k1, yo, k1, sk2p, k1) 10 (10, 12, 12) times, (yo, k1) 2 times, ssk, k1, turn (8 sts rem unworked).

Row 4: P69 (69, 81, 81), turn (8 sts rem unworked).

Row 5: K1, k2tog, k1, (yo, k1, yo, k1, sk2p, k1) 10 (10, 12, 12) times, yo, k1, turn (12 sts rem unworked).

Row 6: P61 (61, 73, 73) turn (12 sts rem unworked).

Row 7: K1, yo, k1, sk2p, k1, (yo, k1, yo, k1, sk2p, k1) 8 (8, 10 10) times, (yo, k1) 2 times, ssk, k1, turn (14 sts rem unworked).

Row 8: P57 (57, 69, 69), turn (14 sts rem unworked).

Row 9: K1, k2tog, k1, (yo, k1, yo, k1, sk2p, k1) 8 (8, 10, 10) times, yo, k1, turn (18 sts rem unworked).

Row 10: P49 (49, 61, 61), turn (18 sts rem unworked).

Row 11: K1, yo, k1, sk2p, k1, (yo, k1, yo, k1, sk2p, k1) 6 (6, 8, 8) times, (yo, k1) 2 times, ssk, k1, turn (20 sts rem unworked).

Row 12: P45 (45, 57, 57) turn (20 sts rem unworked).

Row 13: K1, k2tog, k1, (yo, k1, yo, k1, sk2p, k1) 6 (6, 8, 8) times, yo, k1, turn (24 sts rem unworked).

Row 14: P37 (37, 49, 49) turn (24 sts rem unworked).

Row 15: K1, yo, k1, sk2p, k1, (yo, k1, yo, k1, sk2p, k1) 4 (4, 6, 6) times, (yo, k1) 2 times, ssk, k1, turn (26 sts rem unworked).

Row 16: P33 (33, 45, 45) turn (26 sts rem unworked).

Row 17: K1, k2tog, k1, (yo, k1, yo, k1, sk2p, k1) 4 (4, 6, 6) times, yo, k1, turn (30 sts rem unworked).

Row 18: P25 (25, 37, 37) turn (30 sts rem unworked).

Row 19: K1, yo, k1, sk2p, k1, (yo, k1, yo, k1, sk2p, k1) 2 (2, 4, 4) times, (yo, k1) 2 times, ssk, k1, turn (32 sts rem unworked).

Row 20: P21 (21, 33, 33) turn (32 sts rem unworked).

Row 21: K1, k2tog, k1, (yo, k1, yo, k1, sk2p, k1) 2 (2, 4, 4) times, yo, k1, turn (36 sts rem unworked).

Row 22: P13 (13, 25, 25) turn (36 sts rem unworked).

Sizes Small and Medium Only:
Row 23: K1, yo, k1, sk2p, k1, yo, k1, yo, k1, ssk, k1, turn (38 sts rem unworked).

Row 24: P9, turn (38 sts rem unworked).

Row 25: K1, k2tog, k1, (yo, k1, yo, k1, sk2p, k1) 7 times, end k1.

Row 26: P84.

Sizes Large and X-Large Only:
Row 23: K1, yo, k1, sk2p, k1, (yo, k1, yo, k1, sk2p, k1) 2 times, yo, k1, yo, k1, ssk, k1, turn (38 sts rem unworked).

Row 24: P21 turn (38 sts rem unworked).

Row 25: K1, k2tog, k1, (yo, k1, yo, k1, sk2p, k1) 2 times, yo, k1, turn (42 sts rem unworked).

Row 26: P13 turn (42 sts rem unworked).

Row 27: K1, yo, k1, sk2p, k1, yo, k1, yo, k1, ssk, k1, turn (44 sts rem unworked).

Row 28: P9, turn (44 sts rem unworked).

Row 29: K1, k2tog, k1, (yo, k1, yo, k1, sk2p, k1) 8 times, end k1.

Row 30: P96.

All Sizes:
Begin Body:
Change to longer needle as stitches are sufficiently increased.

Set-up round 1: *K1, yo, k5, yo, PM, k1, yo, k2, k2tog, k1, (yo, k1, yo, k1, sk2p, k1) 4 (4, 5, 5) times, yo, k1, yo, k1, ssk, k2, yo, PM, repeat from * once more, last marker placed is for beginning of round—92 (92, 104, 104) sts. Join to work in the round.

Set-up round 2: Knit around.

Work chart 2 rounds 1–12 2 (3, 3, 4) times, then repeat rounds 1–9 once more, working chart between each set of markers around, repeating highlighted sts as needed in each section—276 (324, 336, 384) sts total, divided on the needle as follows: Small: 54/84/54/84, Medium: 66/96/66/96, Large: 66/102/66/102, X-Large: 78/114/78/114.*

Next round: Slip beginning of round marker, k193 (229, 235, 271), slipping marker when you come to it. Bind off the next 83 (95, 101, 113) sts. You will need to remove beginning of round marker and knit the 1st st of next round to bind off last st. Do not replace the beginning of round marker. Break yarn and set piece aside. Work left sleeve and body.

left sleeve and body

Work as for right sleeve and body to *.

Next round: Slip beginning of round marker, k55 (67, 67, 79), slipping marker when you come to it. Bind off the next 83 (95, 101, 113) sts (up to next marker), remove marker, knit to end of round.

join body sections

With RS facing, slip the next 55 (67, 67, 79) sts of left sleeve and body to 3.5mm (size 4 U.S.) 60" needle (slip all markers when you come to them). With RS facing, slip held 193 (229, 235, 271) sts of right front and sleeve to same needle. Slip remaining 138 (162, 168, 192) sts of left sleeve and body to needle—386 (458, 470, 542) total sts.

Next round: *K1, yo, k2, k2tog, k1, (yo, k1, yo, k1, sk2p, k1) 8 (9, 9, 12) times, yo, remove marker, k2tog, (yo, k1, sk2p, k1, yo, k1) 8 (9, 9, 12) times, yo, k1, ssk, k2, yo, slip marker. Work chart 2 row 11 to next marker, slip marker; repeat from * once more—392 (464, 476, 548) sts.

Next round: Knit around.

You should have 4 markers placed (including the beginning of round marker) with sts divided on the needle as follows: Small: 110/86/110/86, Medium: 134/98/134/98, Large: 134/104/134/104, X-Large: 158/116/158/116.

Work chart 2 rounds 1–10, working chart between each set of markers around, repeating highlighted sts as needed in each section—432 (504, 516, 588) sts.

Remove all markers but beginning of round marker on round 10.

Work chart 3 rounds 1–9 over all sts. Bind off loosely knitwise, using lace bind off (see page 20), on round 10.

FINISHING

Sew sleeve seams. Sew center back seam. Weave in all ends.

Block piece to measurements.

Birch Jacket Chart 1

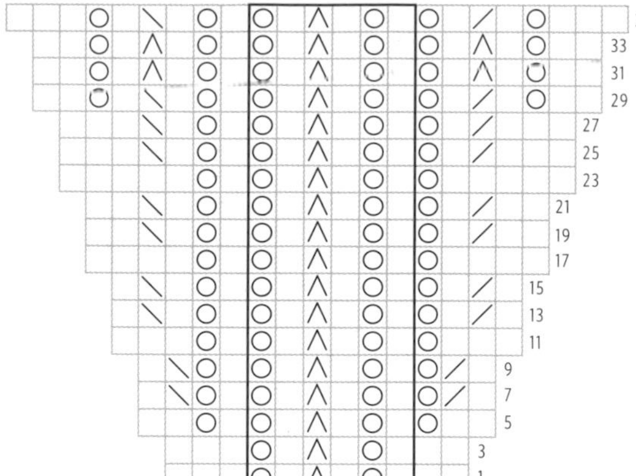

- RS: knit
  WS: purl
- RS: yo
  WS: yo
- RS: k2tog
  WS: p2tog
- RS: ssk
  WS: p2tog, tbl
- RS: sl1, k2tog, psso
  WS: sl1, wyif, p2tog, tbl, psso
- RS: gray no stitch
  WS: gray no stitch
- repeat

Birch Jacket Chart 2

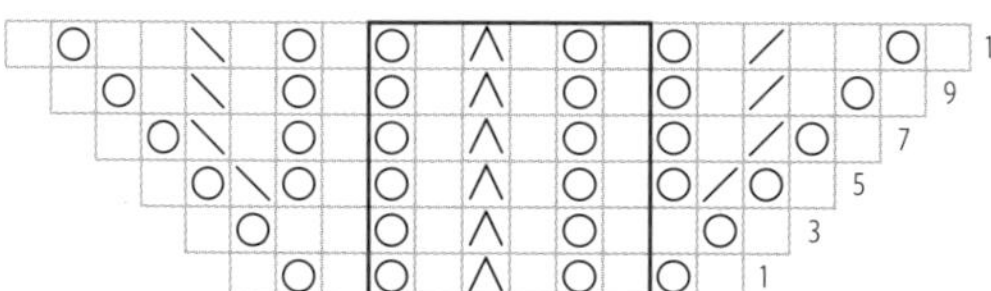

- RS: knit
  WS: purl
- RS: yo
  WS: yo
- RS: k2tog
  WS: p2tog
- RS: ssk
  WS: p2tog, tbl
- RS: sl1, k2tog, psso
  WS: sl1, wyif, p2tog, tbl, psso
- RS: gray no stitch
  WS: gray no stitch
- repeat

Only odd-numbered rows/rounds are charted. All even-numbered rows are purl across. All even-numbered rounds are knit around.

Birch Jacket Chart 3

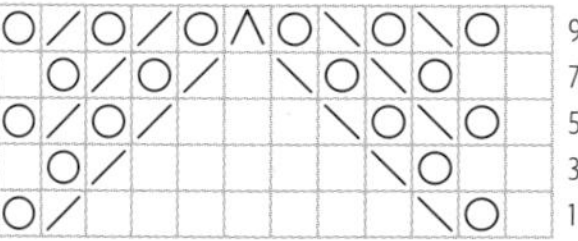

- RS: knit
  WS: purl
- RS: yo
  WS: yo
- RS: k2tog
  WS: p2tog
- RS: ssk
  WS: p2tog, tbl
- RS: sl1, k2tog, psso
  WS: sl1, wyif, p2tog, tbl, psso

Birch Schematics

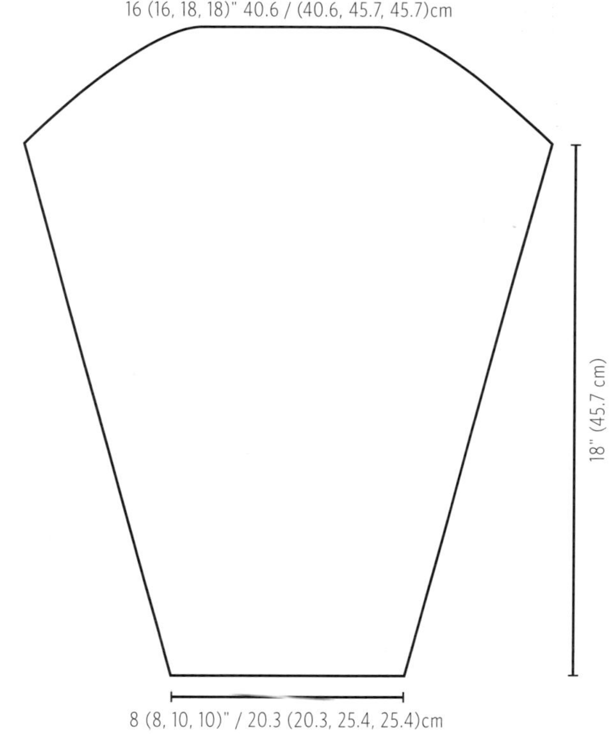

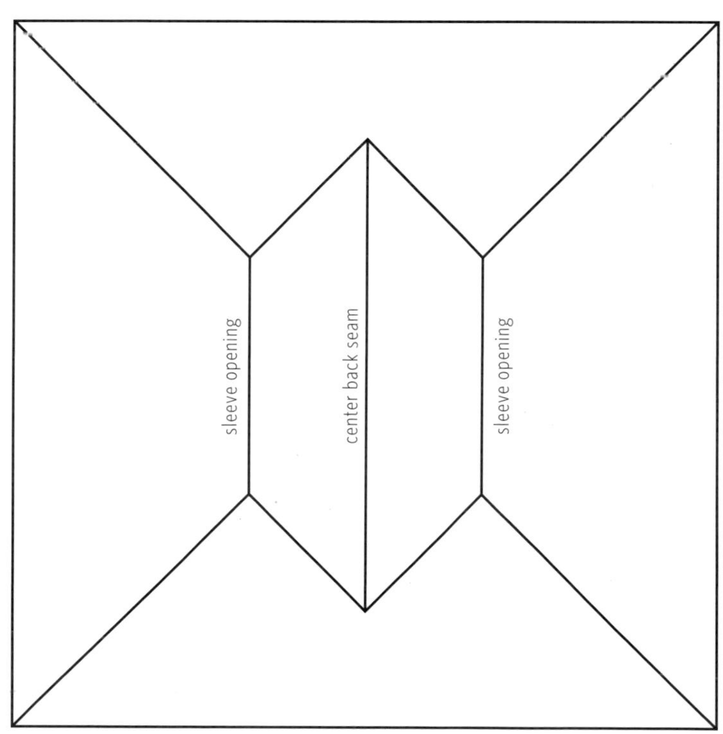

moondance shrug

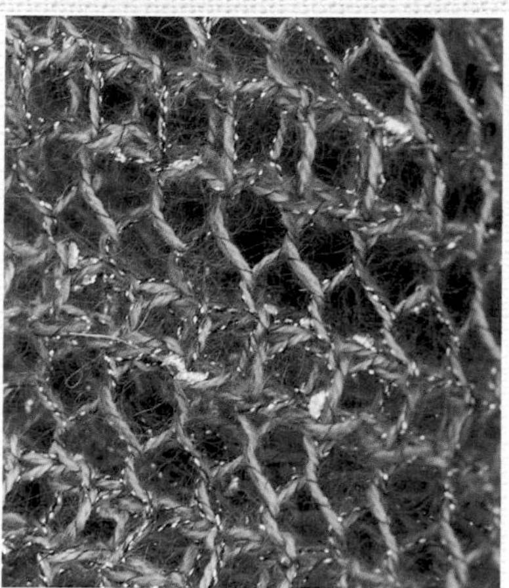

THIS SHRUG STARTS WITH A BASIC SQUARE. Add sleeves and a little seam, and you have a great jacket! I chose to knit this in Gioiello, a shimmering mohair blend, which adds a nice bit of luxe to the garment. Because it is knit out of gauge, at a needle size much larger than you would normally use for this yarn, it is essential that you wash and block your gauge before measuring! The swatch will grow up to 30 percent after blocking. The basic element of this piece is a 32 x 32-inch (81.3 x 81.3cm) square, so feel free to try out different yarns and gauges to make your own. Because of the selvedge stitch (see box below), picking up stitches for the band is easy—just pick up one stitch in every selvedge stitch.

SIZES

Small (Medium, Large, X-Large)

FINISHED MEASUREMENTS

Bust 36 (40, 44, 48)"/91.5 (101.5, 112, 122)cm

MATERIALS AND TOOLS

Filatura Di Crosa Gioiello (30% kid mohair, 30% extrafine merino wool, 20% polyamide, 10% cotton, 10% polyester; 1.75oz/50g = 220yds/200m): 3 (3, 4, 4) skeins, color #67—approx 450 (500, 550, 600)yds/411.5 (457, 503, 548.5)m of sock weight yarn (1)

Knitting needles: 5.5mm (size 9 U.S.) 32" circular or longer or size to obtain gauge

Tapestry needle

GAUGE

13 sts/16 rows = 4"/10cm over Fagoted Rib pattern

Always take time to check your gauge.

Notes

Body and sleeves are worked back and forth in rows on circular needle.

Edging is worked in rounds.

PATTERN STITCHES

fagoted rib pattern worked over a repeat of 4 + 2 sts

Row 1 (RS): K1, (k2, yo, ssk) repeat across, end bring yarn to front between the needles, slip last stitch.

Repeat row 1.

what's a selvedge stitch?

A selvedge stitch makes the edges of your piece smooth and even. This makes your finishing steps, picking up stitches, or seaming much easier. It's a good habit to get into for most of your knitting. There are several ways to do the selvedge stitch, but I prefer the knit selvedge. Simply end every row by slipping the last stitch with the yarn in front. Start every row by knitting the first stitch.

INSTRUCTIONS

Cast on 102 (110, 118, 126) sts.

Begin Fagoted Rib Pattern

Row 1 (RS): K1, (k2, yo, ssk) repeat across, end bring yarn to front between the needles, slip last stitch.

Repeat row 1 for 128 (136, 144, 152) rows, or until piece measures 32 (34, 36, 38)"/81.5 (86.5, 91.5, 96.5)cm from cast on, lightly stretched. Bind off loosely knitwise.

Block piece to 32 (34, 36, 38)"/81.5 (86.5, 91.5, 96.5)cm square.

sleeve

With RS facing, pick up and knit 102 (110, 118, 126) sts evenly across cast on edge.

Row 1 (WS): K2tog across—51 (55, 59, 63) sts.

Rows 2 and 3: Knit.

Row 4 (decrease): K1, ssk, knit to last 3 sts, k2tog, k1—49 (53, 57, 61) sts.

Rows 5–7: Knit.

Repeat the last 6 rows, decreasing 1 st each end every 6th row, 7 times more—35 (39, 43, 47) sts rem.

Bind off loosely knitwise.

Repeat for other sleeve.

Sew sleeve seam from wrist to body join.

edging

With RS facing, pick up and knit 64 (68, 72, 76) sts along lower body opening, working from left sleeve seam to right sleeve seam. Pick up and knit 64 (68, 72, 76) sts along upper body opening, working back to right sleeve seam—128 (136, 144, 152) sts. Place marker and join to work in the round.

Round 1: Purl around.

Round 2: Knit around.

Repeat Rounds 1 and 2.

Bind off loosely knitwise using lace bind off (see page 20) on round 5.

FINISHING

Weave in all ends.

Block piece to finished measurements.

Moondance Shrug Schematic

motifs for exploration

Lace knitting offers so many creative opportunities for you to explore! In this section, you'll find six additional motifs that have all been charted with triangle shaping and can be used in any of the patterns in this book that use the triangle base, such as the Dahlia Shawl (page 98) or the Poinsettia Jacket (page 72), or in your own personal projects.

The swatches have all been worked as a top-down triangle shawl. To complete the shawl, work the instructions for your chosen motif, then follow the directions on page 125. Grab your needles and yarn, and enjoy!

Butterfly Triangle

For the Butterfly Triangle, which is a base of 4 sts, work as follows:

We start the shawl with a tab, which through the magic of knitting will become the edge stitches of the shawl (see "Working a Right Triangle" on page 26 for more information). Traditionally, the tab and edge stitches are worked in garter stitch; however, I like to work them in stockinette stitch. You will find that because of the inherent curl in stockinette stitch, the 4-stitch edge looks like an attached I-cord, and blends in well with the stockinette stitch-based lace motifs shown here. If you prefer the look of a garter stitch edge, simply work the tab as written, substituting garter stitch for stockinette stitch.

Instructions

Cast on 4 sts.

Work 7 rows stockinette st. (1st row is ws row)

Butterfly Triangle Motif

Butterfly Triangle Chart 1

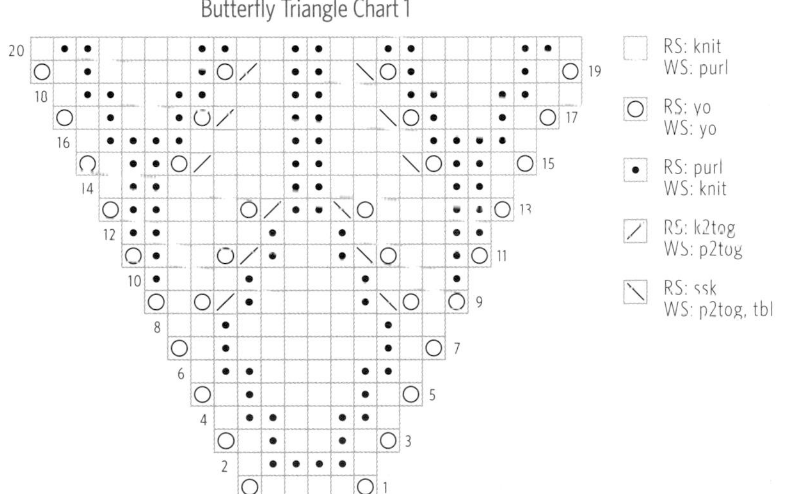

Next row (RS): K4, pick up and knit 5 sts in left selvedge edge, pick up and knit 4 sts in cast on sts—13 sts total. Turn.

Next row (WS): P4, PM, p2, PM, p1, PM, p2, PM, p4.

Next row: k4, (SM, yo, k2, yo, SM), k1, repeat between ( )'s once more, end k4—17 sts total.

Next row: Purl across.

Now you can begin working charts 1 and 2 (see above and on page 120).

Butterfly Triangle Chart 2

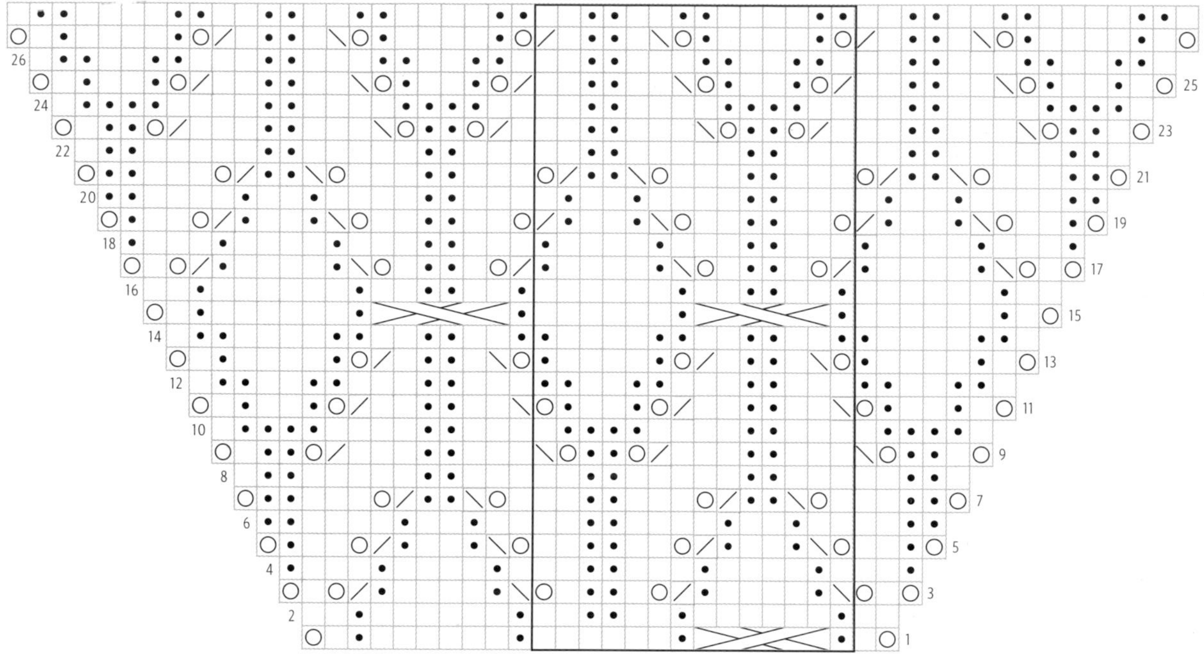

RS: knit
WS: purl

RS: yo
WS: yo

RS: purl
WS: knit

RS: k2tog
WS: p2tog

RS: ssk
WS: p2tog, tbl

RS: 2/2/2 LPC
WS: 2/2/2 LPC

RS: 2/2/2 RPC
WS: 2/2/2 RPC

repeat

Additional Motifs

Here you'll find charts for five more motifs: The Long Flower, Small Fountain, Small Tulip, Water Lily Triangle, and Japanese Cables & Lace. While the Butterfly Triangle motif is based on an even number of stitches, these motifs have an odd number of stitches in the repeat. Simply begin with the instructions below, then continue with the chart for the motif of your choice.

All motifs have a base of 1 st.

Instructions

All WS rows are purl, unless otherwise noted.

Cast on 4 sts.

Work 5 rows stockinette st (1st row is ws row).

Next row (RS): K4, pick up and knit 3 sts in left selvedge edge, pick up and knit 4 sts in cast on sts—11 sts total. Turn.

Next row (WS): P4, PM, p1, PM, p1, PM, p1, place marker, p4.

Now you can begin working charts as instructed.

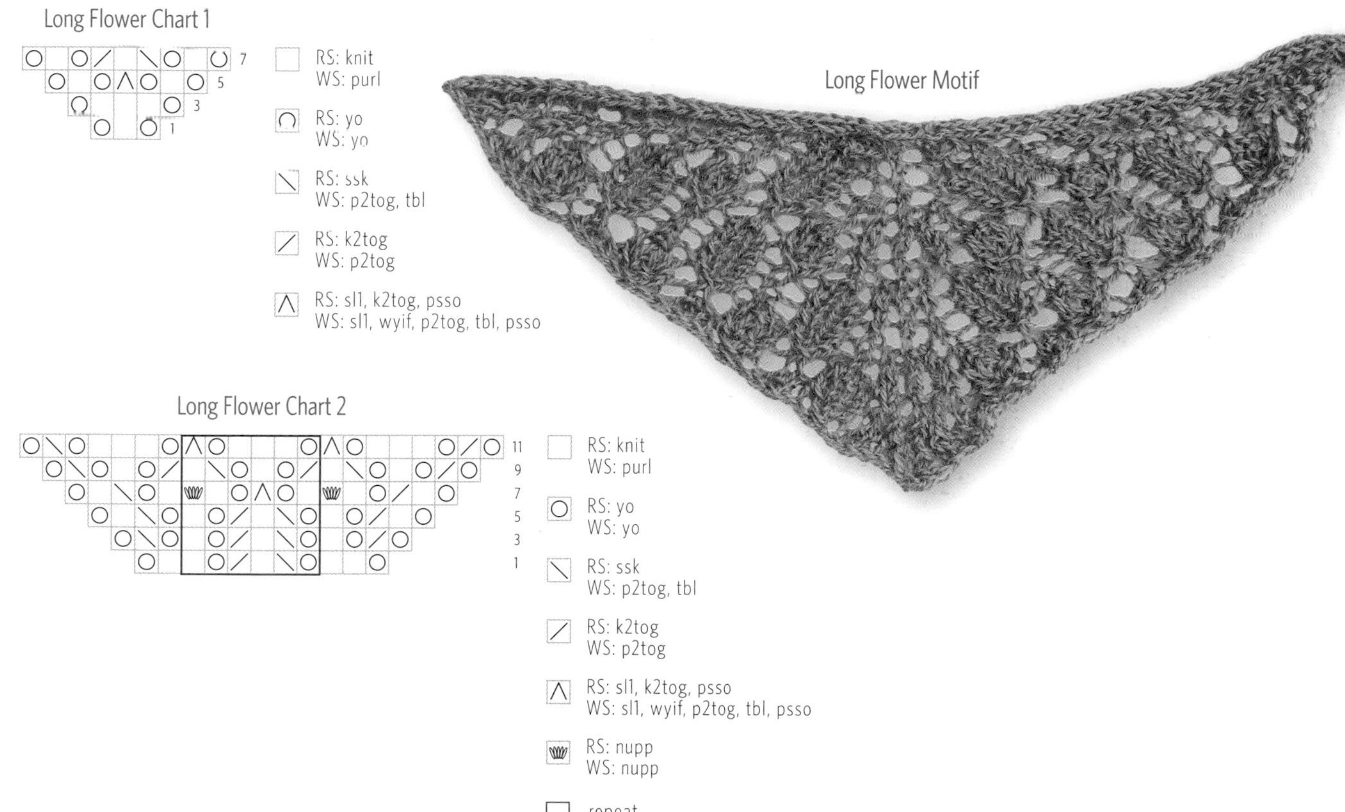

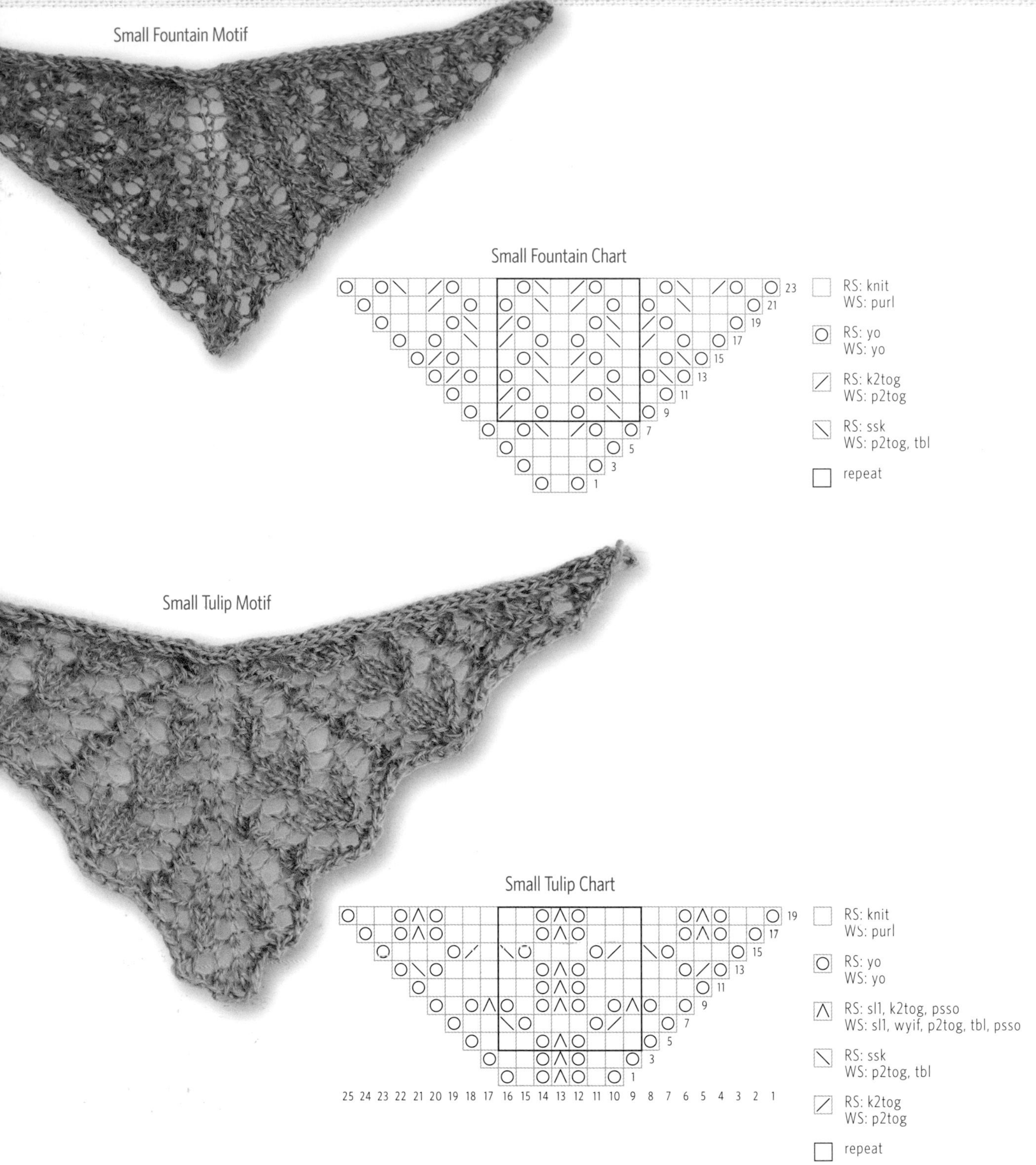
Small Fountain Motif
Small Fountain Chart
RS: knit
WS: purl
RS: yo
WS: yo
RS: k2tog
WS: p2tog
RS: ssk
WS: p2tog, tbl
repeat
Small Tulip Motif
Small Tulip Chart
25 24 23 22 21 20 19 18 17 16 15 14 13 12 11 10 9 8 7 6 5 4 3 2 1
RS: knit
WS: purl
RS: yo
WS: yo
RS: sl1, k2tog, psso
WS: sl1, wyif, p2tog, tbl, psso
RS: ssk
WS: p2tog, tbl
RS: k2tog
WS: p2tog
repeat

Water Lily Triangle Motif

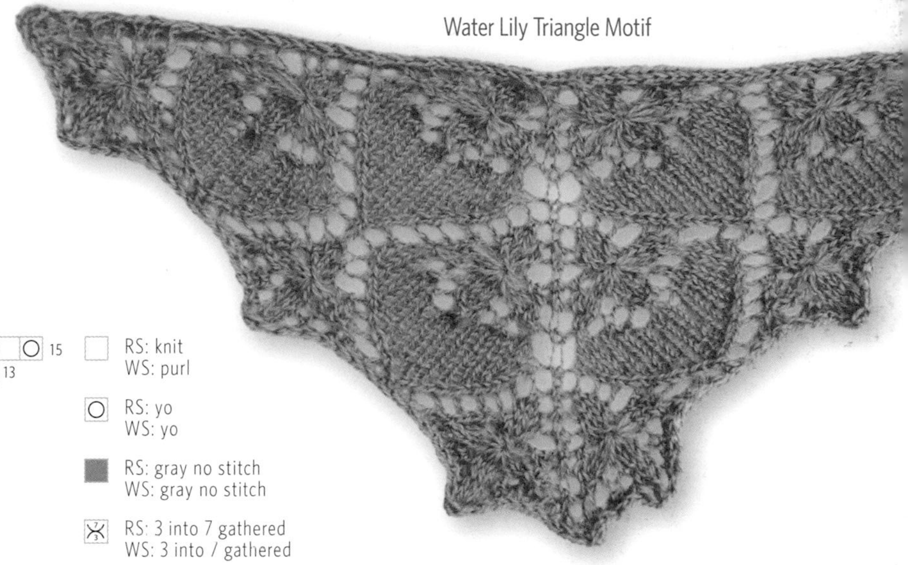

Water Lily Triangle Chart 1

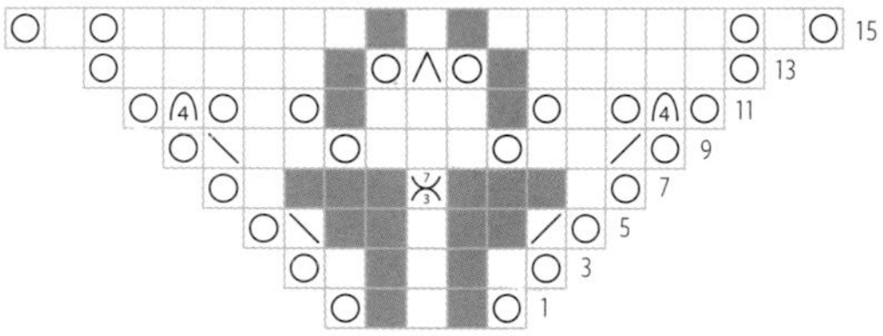

- RS: knit
  WS: purl
- RS: yo
  WS: yo
- RS: gray no stitch
  WS: gray no stitch
- RS: 3 into 7 gathered
  WS: 3 into / gathered
- RS: k2tog
  WS: p2tog
- RS: ssk
  WS: p2tog, tbl
- RS: sl1, k2tog, psso
  WS: sl1, wyif, p2tog, tbl, psso
- RS: 4 into 1 decrease
  WS: k4tog tbl

Water Lily Triangle Chart 2

- RS: knit
  WS: purl
- RS: yo
  WS: yo
- RS: gray no stitch
  WS: gray no stitch
- RS: 3 into 7 gathered
  WS: 3 into 7 gathered
- RS: k2tog
  WS: p2tog
- RS: ssk
  WS: p2tog, tbl
- RS: sl1, k2tog, psso
  WS: sl1, wyif, p2tog, tbl, psso
- repeat
- RS: 4 into 1 decrease
  WS: k4tog tbl

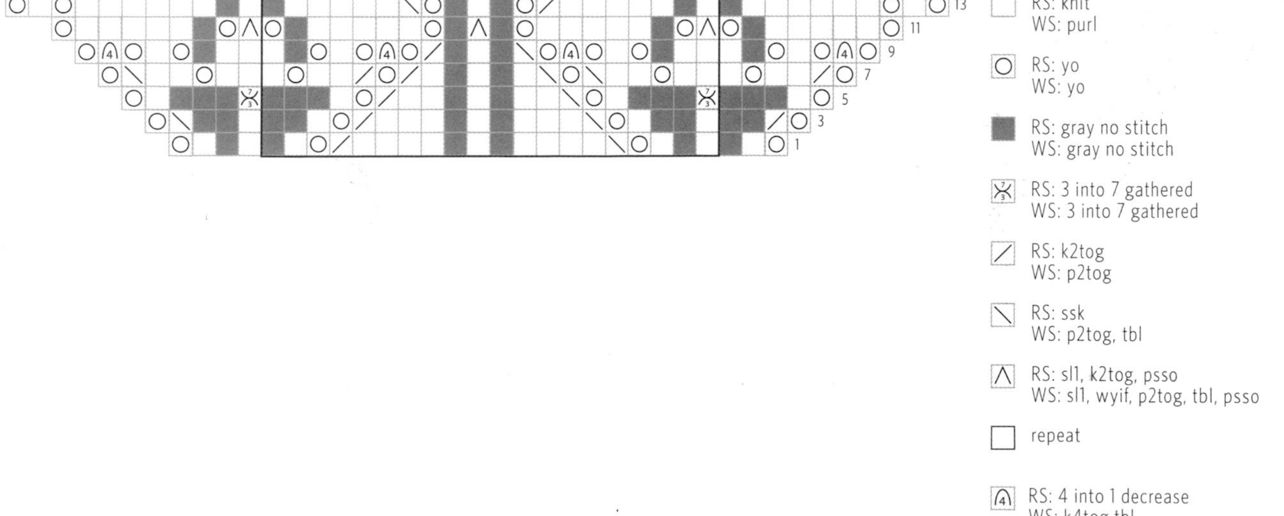

Japanese Cables & Lace Chart 1

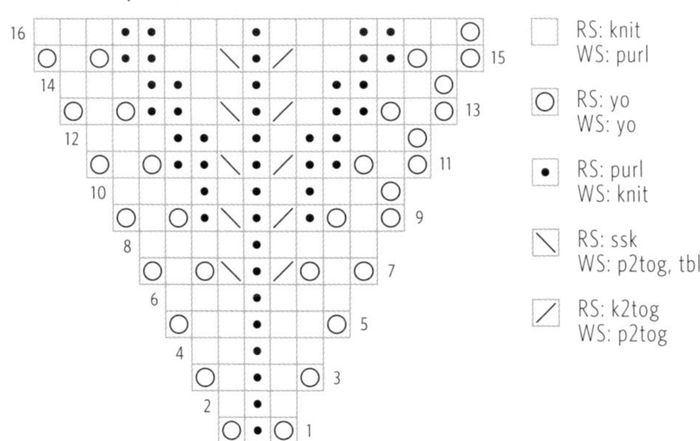

Japanese Cables & Lace Chart 2

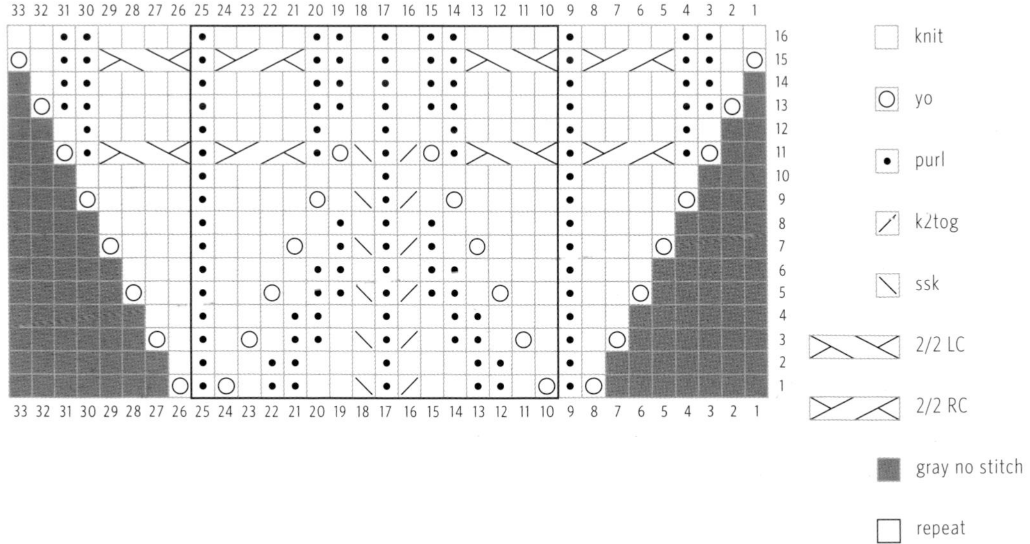

Japanese Cables & Lace Motif

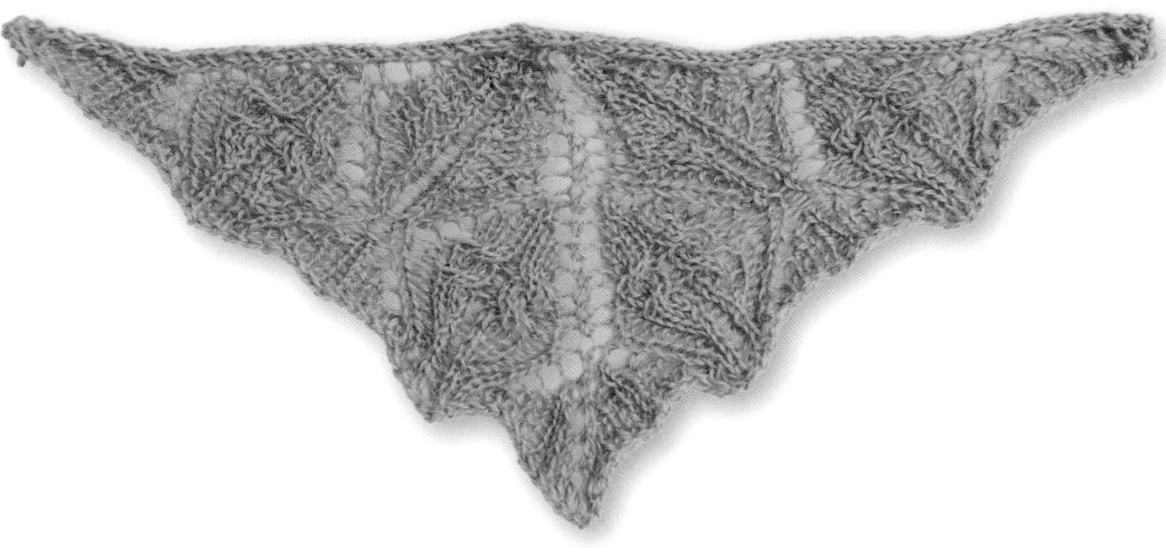

Working charts for a triangle shawl:

You now have the stitches arranged on the needles as follows: 4 edge stitches, 1 (2) triangle stitch, 1 spine stitch, 1 (2) triangle stitch, 4 edge stitches. The 4 edge stitches on either end are not charted, and will be worked in stockinette stitch throughout. The center spine stitch is also not charted and will be worked in stockinette stitch throughout. (It is also important to note that the stockinette stitch should always be isolated, sitting all by itself in between 2 markers!) That leaves the 1 or 2 triangle stitches on either side of that spine stitch. You will work the charts in those sections, therefore repeating the chart 2 times in each row. When necessary, two charts have been given. Chart 1 is the setup, and is only worked 1 time. Chart 2 is the repeat, and you can work all the rows of chart 2 as many times as you like, repeating the highlighted stitches as necessary to the marker, until the shawl is your desired size.

All the swatches are worked in Rowan Fine Lace (80% Alpaca 20% Merino; 50 gm/1.76 oz.= 400/437 yd.) using a 2.25mm/U.S. 9 needle.

KNITTING ABBREVIATIONS

ABBREVIATION	DESCRIPTION	ABBREVIATION	DESCRIPTION	ABBREVIATION	DESCRIPTION	ABBREVIATION	DESCRIPTION
[ ]	work instructions within brackets as many times as directed	fl	front loop(s)	pop	popcorn	sl1p	slip 1 purlwise
( )	work instructions within parentheses as many times as directed	foll	follow/follows/ following	prev	previous	ss	slip stitch (Canadian)
* *	repeat instructions following the asterisks as directed	g	gram	psso	pass slipped stitch over	ssk	slip, slip, knit these 2 stitches together—a decrease
*	repeat instructions following the single asterisk as directed	inc	increase/increases/ increasing	pwise	purlwise	sssk	slip, slip, slip, knit 3 stitches together
"	inches	k or K	knit	p2tog	purl 2 stitches together	st(s)	stitch(es)
alt	alternate	kwise	knitwise	rem	remain/remaining	St st	stockinette stitch/ stocking stitch
approx	approximately	k2tog	knit 2 stitches together	rep	repeat(s)	tbl	through back loop
beg	begin/beginning	LH	left hand	rev St st	reverse stockinette stitch	tog	together
bet	between	lp(s)	loop(s)	RH	right hand	w & t	wrap and turn
BO	bind off	m	meter(s)	rnd(s)	round(s)	WS	wrong side
CC	contrasting color	MC	main color	RS	right side	wyib	with yarn in back
cm	centimeter(s)	mm	millimeter(s)	sk	skip	wyif	with yarn in front
cn	cable needle	M1	make 1 stitch	skp	slip, knit, pass stitch over—one stitch decreased	yd(s)	yard(s)
CO	cast on	M1 p-st	make 1 purl stitch	sk2p	slip 1, knit 2 together, pass slip stitch over the knit 2 together; 2 stiches have been decreased	yfwd	yarn forward
cont	continue	oz	ounce(s)	sl	slip	yo	yarn over
dec	decrease/decreases/ decreasing	p or P	purl	sl st	slip stitch(es)	yon	yarn over needle
dpn	double pointed needle(s)	PM	place marker	sl1k	slip 1 knitwise	yrn	yarn around needle

YARN WEIGHTS

YARN WEIGHT SYMBOL & CATEGORY NAMES	0 lace	1 super fine	2 fine	3 light	4 medium	5 bulky	6 super bulky
TYPE OF YARNS IN CATEGORY	Fingering 10-count crochet thread	Sock, Fingering, Baby	Sport, Baby	DK, Light Worsted	Worsted, Afghan, Aran	Chunky, Craft, Rug	Bulky, Roving

Source: Craft Yarn Council of America's www.YarnStandards.com

KNITTING NEEDLE SIZE CHART

METRIC (MM)	US	UK/CANADIAN
2.0	0	14
2.25	1	13
2.75	2	12
3.0	–	11
3.25	3	10
3.5	4	–
3.75	5	9
4.0	6	8
4.5	7	7
5.0	8	6
5.5	9	5
6.0	10	4
6.5	10½	3
7.0	–	2
7.5	–	1
8.0	11	0
9.0	13	00
10.0	15	000
12.0	17	–
16.0	19	–
19.0	35	–
25.0	50	–

About the Author

Brooke Nico lives in Kirkwood, MO, a lovely area with a small-town feel, and a great place to raise kids. It's there that she founded Kirkwood Knittery, which she now runs with business partner Robyn Schrager. A seamstress all her life, Brooke learned to sew her own clothes early to fit her tall, thin frame. In 2000, she taught herself to knit and fell in love with the concept of creating her own fabric while creating a garment. Brooke travels and teaches at knitting events around the country, and her designs have been published in *Sock Yarn Studio* (Lark Crafts, 2012), *One + One Scarves, Shawls & Shrugs* (Lark Crafts, 2012), and *One + One Hats* (Lark Crafts, 2012). Her friends describe her as creative, sharp, and witty. She often talks to her knitting (she swears it answers back!), and she loves shoes, handbags, and coffee. Brooke's designs can be found online at www.kirkwoodknittery.com.

Acknowledgments

I am so fortunate to work in this wonderful industry, full of enthusiastic and creative people. There are so many people to thank, but I must start by thanking the woman who recognized my design aesthetic and gave me my first opportunity to share my designs with the public, Trisha Malcolm. Her continued support and trust have enabled me to push myself and to expand my career. The wonderful designers and teachers I get to work with throughout the year are a constant source of encouragement. Carol Sulcoski has always been a wonderful source of support and encouragement for me.

Each day, I go to work at my yarn store, Kirkwood Knittery, and get to meet new knitters, from beginners full of energy for their new craft to regular customers eager to cast on a new project. Every one of you has inspired and energized me in your own way, but especially our "knit night gang" and our great team of co-workers, Nadine Rinehart, Franni Goette, and Rachel Bowler. I have loved sharing the progress of this book with you and getting feedback and insight with each step of the way. My great team of knitters, Emily Hixson, Franni Goette, Rachel Bowler, Susan Monroe, and Christine Yokoyama, have my undying gratitude. My business partner and co-owner of Kirkwood Knittery, Robyn Schrager, has been an invaluable resource. Robyn and I enjoy bouncing ideas off each other, and she always pushes me to be my best. Her at times brutal honesty is always refreshing and helpful!

My family has tolerated my inane ramblings and my answering their questions with "100, 101, 102..." as I count my stitches. They have patiently waited until I "get to the end of my row" for my attention. For that I am incredibly grateful. Jason, Austin, Caleb, and Peyton, none of this would be possible without your support and encouragement. My parents who encouraged me and my siblings to always be our best selves deserve my gratitude.

And finally, to my editor, Shannon, who took those same ramblings and put them into a cohesive whole, thank you very much! Everyone at Lark helped me to find my way through this process, from taking my thoughts and creating a clear direction for this book to this final product.

Index

Belly button cast on, 17
Charts, how to work, 14
Gauge, 10
Knitting abbreviations, 126
Lace bind off, 20
Lace knitting, fixing mistakes, 20
Lace yarn, 8
Needle sizes, 127
Nupps, 18
Pattern stitches
- butterflies lace, 53
- estonian heart motif, 57
- fagoted rib, 115
- fagot stitch, 109
- floral diamonds, 41
- floral diamonds lace, 36
- star stitch, 60

Provisional cast on, 16
Right triangle, knitting a, 26
Short rows, 19
Special abbreviations
- 2-2-2 LPC, 53
- 2-2-2 RPC, 53
- 2/2, 57, 60
- 4 into 1 decrease, 67
- hook 3 stitches, 104
- mock cable, 47

Wrap and turn, 19
Yarn weight, 127

Editors: Shannon Quinn-Tucker
& Amanda Carestio
Art Director: Shannon Yokeley
Designer: Kara Plikaitis
Illustrator: Orrin Lundgren
Photographer: Carrie Hoge
Cover Designer: Shannon Yokeley